Common Issues We Face in Life

Addressing the Issues from a Biblical Perspective

Dr. Nicolas Ellen

Common Issues We Face in Life

Addressing the Issues from a Biblical Perspective

Readers may order copies by visiting www.mycounselingcorner.com.

Published and Printed By Expository Counseling Center
Houston, Texas

Unless otherwise noted, scripture references are taken from the New American Standard Bible. © The Lockman Foundation, 1960, 1962, 1963, 1968, 1971, 1972, 1973, 1975, 1977.

Publisher's Cataloging in Publication

Ellen, Nicolas: *Common Issues We Face in Life*
   1. Counseling 2. Christian Counseling 3. Christianity 4. Discipleship

ISBN 978-0-9779692-2-7

Common Issues We Face in Life
Table of Contents

Common Issues We Face in Life

Week One   **Section One: Pride/Humility**

Week Two   **Section Two: The Point of Choice**

Week Three   **Section Three: Idolatrous Lust**

Week Four   **Section Four: Worry**

Week Five   **Section Five: The Fear of Man**

Week Six   **Section Six: Anger/Learning Contentment**

Week Seven   **Section Seven: Self-Esteem, Self- Image, Self-Love**

Week Eight   **Section Eight: Trials/ Suffering/Depression**

Week Nine   **Section Nine: How to Deal with The Past**

Week Ten   **Section Ten: Decision Making**

Week Eleven   **Section Eleven: Living by Purpose**

Week Twelve   **Section Twelve: The Cycle of Relationships**

Week Thirteen   **Section Thirteen: Abuse, Separation, Divorce, Remarriage**

Week Fourteen   **Section Fourteen: Death, Grief, Despair, Biblical View of Illness, Psychotropic Drugs and Biblical Counseling**

Section One

Pride/Humility

Understanding Pride

Key Point: Pride is at the root of every sin you commit and is at the core of the problems we have with people and circumstances. Therefore, we need to understand the nature of pride if we are going to deal properly with the problems we face with people and circumstances.

I.   The *Principle* of Pride: Pride is mind set on *self* with resistance and or a lack of submission to the will of God. (Romans 8:5-7)

    A. A mind governed by one's owns assessment of self with resistance and or a lack of submission to the will of God. (Luke 18:9-14)

    B. A mind governed by one's own belief system about God, life, and people with resistance and or lack of submission to the will of God. (Proverbs 28:26)

    C. A mind governed by trust, confidence, or dependence in one's own abilities, accomplishments, academics, affluence, associations, or position in life, with resistance and or lack of submission to the will of God . (Daniel 4: 30-37)

    D. A mind governed by service of self , sustaining of self, satisfaction of self, or exalting one's self with resistance and or lack of submission to the will of God. (Genesis 11:1-9)

II.   The *Problem* of Pride: Pride is *detestable* to God and brings *detriment* to you from God when you walk in it. (Proverbs 6:16-17, Psalm 119:21)

    A. Pride is hated by God. (Proverbs 6:16-17)

    B. Pride puts you in opposition to God. (James 4:6)

    C. Pride leads God to bring destruction to your home. (Proverbs 15:25a)

    D. Pride leads to God's judgment of you. (Proverbs 16:5)

III. The *Practice* of Pride: Life is lived being *consumed* with pleasing, providing, or promoting, or one's self with a lack of love for *God* and others. (2 Timothy 3:1-4)

    A. Pride is revealed in one being preoccupied with having their way and using people to get it resulting in confusion disorder and every evil thing in their lives. (James 3:13-16)

    B. Pride is revealed in one having a sense of entitlement to God's comfort while getting anger when God allows discomfort in one's life. (Jonah 4: 5-9)

C. Pride is revealed in one talking in a manner which reveals that they think too highly of themselves. (Psalm 94:4)

D. Pride is revealed in rebellion and or disrespect of God and God-given authority in one's life. (Nehemiah 9:1-26)

IV. **The _Product_ of Pride**: Pride leads to a **_disconnect_** from God, a downfall in your life, and to division with others. (Hosea 7:10, Proverbs 18:12, 29:23, 13:10)

A. Pride hinders you from seeking the Lord. (Hosea 7:10)
B. Pride leads you to be deceived about who you really are. (Jeremiah 49:16)
C. Pride hinders you from genuine improvement. (Proverbs 26:12)
D. Pride brings shame to your life. (Proverbs 11:2)
E. Pride leads you to self-destruction. (Proverbs 16:18)
F. Pride leads you to stir up strife with others. (Proverbs 28:25)

V. **The _Picture_ of Pride:** Pride will **_manifest_** itself in many ways and in various forms:

A. Arrogance – to exaggerate one's own worth/importance.
B. Presumption- to suppose that something is true without checking because you think you know.
C. Unbelief – skepticism of truth presented by God.
D. Self -Protection – keeping yourself from people, places, and things that may hurt you or disappoint you and using that as an excuse not to love.
E. Un-forgiveness – holding a grudge against someone, not setting them free from the wrong they have committed against you even though they have sought your forgiveness.
F. Unbiblical Control – seeking to regulate what people think, say and do according to your personal standards and agenda and not God's Will.
G. Self-preoccupation – preoccupation with what happens to you, through you and for you.
H. Blame Shifting – blaming your sin on the negligence of someone else or circumstances perceived as beyond your control.
I. Grumbling- unthankful in your situation or with people, believing you deserve better or more.
J. Lazy- doing things when you get ready or when you feel like it not when God has commanded.
K. Self-Sufficient- living and believing the lie that you do not need anyone and that you can handle life by yourself.
L. Un-Teachable- unwilling to listen to instruction.
M. Lack of submission- unwilling to follow the instruction.
N. Perfectionism- setting standards that God did not set and seeking to live by them without any failure in them.
O. Pity Party- always focusing on how bad you are and how bad you fail and feeling sorrow for yourself as a result.

P. Resisting Accountability- unwilling to answer to people and to be open to people who can help keep you from the people, places, products, or perspectives that lead you into sin or help you to confess, repent and replace sin with right living.

Q. Defensive attitude- seeking to escape or avoid criticism through some rationalization, justification or denial.

(Portions of insight in this list came from the booklet From Pride To Humility by Stuart Scott pp. 6-10)

VI. The *Process* to Put Away Pride (Proverbs 28:13-14)

A. Examine Yourself (Proverbs 14:8).

  1. What has God said to me that I cannot accept?

  2. Who do I compare myself with?

  3. What standards of thinking, behaving and living govern my life?

  4. Do I live by what I feel or what God says?

  5. What areas of my life have I chosen not to submit to God?

B. Examine Your Relationships (Romans 12:9-21).

  1. How often do I confess my faults to a person I have offended?

  2. How often do I confess my hurts to a person I have offended?

  3. Is my anger toward my family, friends, co-workers and church members pleasing to God or displeasing to God?

  4. Am I critical of family, friends, co-workers, and church leaders who do not do things according to my standards?

  5. Do I give according to my feelings or God's standards?

  6. Do I love according to my standards or God's standards?

C. Examining your response to God given authority (1 Peter 2:13-17).

  1. Am I submitting to my husband according to my standards or God's standards?

  2. Am I submitting to leaders on the job, at church according to my standards or God's standards?

  3. Do I have a Biblical reason not to submit?

D. How Do We Deal With It?   (Proverbs 28:13-14)

   1. Identify key areas where you have pride:

      a. Family

      b. Friends

      c. Work

      d. Finances

      e. Reputation

      f. Entertainment

   2. Ask yourself, "Am I willing to live up under God's authority in this area of my life?"

   3. Confess to God your sin of pride in this area.

   4. Ask God to give you a desire and will to repent in this area.

   5. Learn God's truth in the area and meditate on it consistently.

   6. Do the hard work of training in God's truth through the help of the Holy Spirit and other believers.

   7. Expect difficulty, hardships, and resistance from all angles.

   8. Allow God's grace, time, and truth to strengthen you as you train through the difficulty, hardship, and resistance.

   9. Find a set of people that will encourage you, keep you accountable and work with you.

   (For more insight on this read the booklet <u>From Pride to Humility</u> by Stuart Scott)

Understanding Humility

Key Point: Humility leads to a life that glorifies God, stability, transformation, and edification of others. If we want this kind of life we need to understand and live a life of humility.

I. **The *Principle* of Humility**: Humility is a mind set on *Christ* with submission to the will of God.
(Romans 8:5-7, Galatians 2:20, 2Corinthians 5: 8-9, 15, Galatians 5:6, 13)

   A. One who is walking in humility is focused on the Person, Practice, Plan, and Precepts of Jesus Christ.

   B. One who is walking in humility recognizes that his life is no longer his but belongs to Jesus Christ.

   C. One who is walking in humility has a life committed to obedience to God in all aspects of life.

   D. One who is walking in humility has a life committed to loving others which works out in   servant-hood towards others.

II. **The *Perspective* of Humility**: One who walks in humility has a right view of *self,* people, life and God as granted by God to see it. (Romans 12:3)

   A. One who is walking in humility sees the greatness of God and the smallness of himself in comparison to God. (Job 42:2-6)

   B. One who is walking in humility sees his sinfulness and is willing to surrender to God for mercy. (Luke 18:9-14)

   C. One who is walking in humility has the right view of his resources and abilities granted by God. (Romans 12:3)

   D. One who is walking in humility has an accurate understanding of his roles, responsibilities in life in relation to God and others. (John 22:22-36)

III. **The *Picture* of Humility**: Humility will manifest itself in many ways and in many forms:

   A. A willingness and action of following the instructions of God.

   B. A willingness and action of submitting to God-ordained authority.

C. A willingness and action of serving others without looking for anything in return.

D. A willingness and action of listening to and acting upon the wise counsel of others.

E. Being faithful, available, and teachable in all aspects of life.

F. Considering the interest of others and acting upon this without looking for anything in return.

G. Accepting what God allows without grumbling or complaining about it.

H. Submitting to what God says without grumbling or complaining about it.

I. Not preoccupied with self and what others think of them but preoccupied with thoughts of God and how to serve others.

IV. **The _Prize_ of Humility**: One who walks in humility can expect God's **_kindness_** and empowerment for sanctification and service. This can be seen in various ways. (James 4:6)

A. Humility can lead to salvation (Job 22:29).

B. Humility can lead to God's justice on your behalf (Psalm 25:9).

C. Humility can lead to God giving you understanding of His Ways (Psalm 25:9).

D. Humility can lead to God-given wisdom (Proverbs 11:2).

E. Humility can lead to God-given honor (Proverbs 29:23).

F. Humility can lead to God's exaltation (Luke 18:14).

G. Humility can lead to God answering yes to your prayer request (2Chronicles 7:14).

H. Humility can lead to God satisfying your desires accordingly (Psalm 145:18-19).

I. Humility can lead to God providing you with inner strength (Psalm 10:17).

(For more insight on this read the booklet From Pride to Humility by Stuart Scott)

V. The *Process* to Humility

A. Examine *Yourself*.

1. What sin has God exposed that I am repenting of right now?

2. In what areas of my life am I obeying God right now?

3. Have I been giving thanks for everything or have I been complaining about people/places/things/circumstances

4. What is preoccupying my thinking (serving or being served?)

B. Examine Your *Relationships*.

1. How often do I confess my sin and seek forgiveness from people I have sinned against?

2. How often do I confess my hurts to people who have offended me?

3. How do I speak the truth in Love to others?

4. Am I encouraging more and criticizing less?

5. Am I serving others consistently or as I feel like it?

6. Am I on the defense when others tell me I am wrong or have sinned?

7. Am I teachable or just able to teach

8. Do I have a hard time accepting being wrong or is becoming easier to deal with?

C. Examine Your Response to *Authority*.

1. How often do I follow the instructions of My Husband?

2. How often do I follow the instructions of leaders on my job, at church, in the government?

3. Do I submit to leaders according to my standards or God's standards?

4. Do I have biblical reasons not follow the instructions given by the authorities over me?

5. How often do I fight against instructions that I don't agree with or don't feel like doing?

6. Do people have to instruct me in a certain way before I submit or do I submit as unto to the Lord?

D. Commit to the put off put on ***process.***

   1. Ask yourself "Am I willing to live up under God's Authority in all areas of my life?"

   2. Confess to God your sin of pride in the areas where you find pride.

   3. Learn how God wants you to walk in those areas of your life by studying God's Word and seeking wise counsel.

   4. Pray for God's Wisdom on how to apply what He gives you to do.

   5. Through the power of the Holy Spirit, and support of other Believers, set goals on a weekly basis for doing what God commanded.

   6. Work daily at accomplishing these goals of obedience.

   7. Expect difficulty and resistance from your flesh the world and the devil.

   8. When you fall get up and keep training in the truth.

   9. Let others support you and hold you accountable.

Section Two

The Point of Choice

Key Point: At the end of the day man only has two choices; to be self-centered or God-centered. This drives every other issue in life man encounters. The more we choose to be self-centered the more we are held captive by our sin. The more we choose to be God-centered we are freed from sin but walk in slavery to God resulting in God's glory and our greatest good. The condition of our lives is determined by the choices we have made in life. Genuine biblical counseling helps individuals to understand this reality and to pursue choice of being God-centered.

I. **We choose to be God-Centered or Self-Centered**. *(Galatians 5:16-25)*
    (See Illustration of Point I)

      a. When we are God-centered we choose to live our lives for God resulting in doing things according to God's standards. (Psalm 119:105)

      b. When we are self-centered we choose to live our lives for ourselves resulting in doing things according to our own agenda. (2Timohty 3:1-4)

      c. When we choose to live for ourselves instead of living for God we will live in slavery to sin. (Proverbs 4:22).

      d. When we choose to live for God instead of living for ourselves we live in slavery to God (Romans 6:22).

Illustration of Point I.

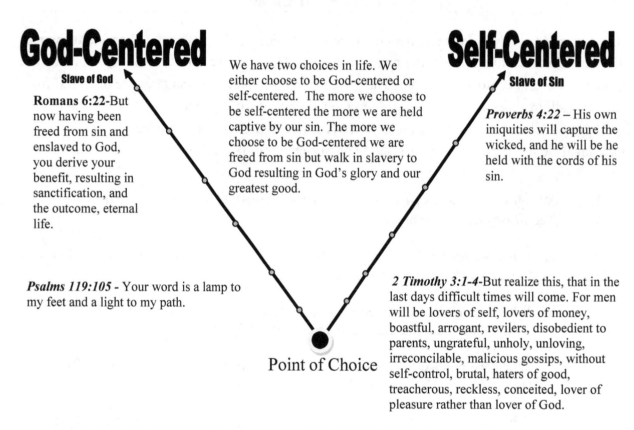

God-Centered
Slave of God

Romans 6:22-But now having been freed from sin and enslaved to God, you derive your benefit, resulting in sanctification, and the outcome, eternal life.

Psalms 119:105 - Your word is a lamp to my feet and a light to my path.

We have two choices in life. We either choose to be God-centered or self-centered. The more we choose to be self-centered the more we are held captive by our sin. The more we choose to be God-centered we are freed from sin but walk in slavery to God resulting in God's glory and our greatest good.

Self-Centered
Slave of Sin

Proverbs 4:22 – His own iniquities will capture the wicked, and he will be he held with the cords of his sin.

Point of Choice

2 Timothy 3:1-4-But realize this, that in the last days difficult times will come. For men will be lovers of self, lovers of money, boastful, arrogant, revilers, disobedient to parents, ungrateful, unholy, unloving, irreconcilable, malicious gossips, without self-control, brutal, haters of good, treacherous, reckless, conceited, lover of pleasure rather than lover of God.

Graphics developed by Cathy Poulos from the presentation "Idols of the Heart," by Mark Dutton, NANC On-the-Road-Training, Track #1, Module #2, November 2003, Houston, TX.

The Point of Choice

II. **Our choices are driven by our thoughts**. *(Romans 8:5)(See illustration of Point II)*

    a. When we are self-centered, our thoughts are dominated by lies and selfish ambition. (James 3:13-16)

    b. As a result of those lies and selfish ambition, our thoughts tend to be driven and reduced to what we have been denied, what we believe we deserve, what we want, what we think we should have or what we think we need. We become friendly with the world and unfriendly with God. (James 4:1-10)

    c. When we are God-centered, our thoughts are dominated by truth and wisdom.(James 3:17-18)

    d. As a result being dominated by truth and wisdom, our thoughts tend be driven by what God commands of us and how to live according to that; We focus on things such as what God promises to do for us and when to expect it. We tend to also focus on what God is doing for us , has done for us as well as what we can be doing for others and how to do it accordingly. (James 3:17-18)

Illustration of Point II.

God-Centered

Self-Centered

Inner Man / **Actions** (left side)

Inner Man / **Actions** (right side)

Point of Choice

Thinking

A mindset that God Wants Us to Develop

James 3:17-18 - The wisdom from above is first pure, then peaceable, gentle, reasonable, full of mercy and good fruits, unwavering, without hypocrisy. And the seed whose fruit is righteousness is sown in peace by those who make peace.

☐ *A mind preoccupied with the truth of God's Word*

☐ *A mind preoccupied with Godly wisdom*

A mindset that God Wants Us to *Avoid*

James 3:15-16 - But if you have bitter jealousy and selfish ambition in your heart, do not be arrogant and so lie against the truth. This wisdom is not from above, but earthly, natural and demonic.

☐ *A mind preoccupied with lies*

☐ *A mind preoccupied with selfish ambition*

Graphics developed by Cathy Poulos from the presentation "The Heart of Man as Presented in the Book of Psalms," by Mark Dutton, Co-Pastor of Faith Baptist Church, Lafayette, IN; NANC certified instructor.

16

The Point of Choice

III. **Our thoughts are motivated by the flesh (sin in our hearts) or by the Holy Spirit Romans 8:1-14** *(See illustration of Point III)*

    a. When our thoughts are motivated by the flesh (sin in our hearts) we are preoccupied with issues such as hedonism (preoccupation with whatever bring me pleasure apart from God), autonomy (independence from authority; not having to answer to any one), materialism (preoccupation with material things), and entitlement (believing I deserve whatever I want or pursue) dominate our thinking.

    b. This leads to further disobedience to God. We will see things such as anger, hatred, immorality, jealousy, abuse, cruelty, lying, selfish ambition, arrogance, rage, sarcasm or selfishness. This leads to a guilty conscience, a fear of God's judgment, and a desire to escape God's judgment resulting in trying to flee from the inevitable consequences of disobedience to God. (2 Timothy 3:1-9, Proverbs 28:1)

    c. When our thoughts are motivated by the Holy Spirit we tend to be preoccupied with a desire to know Jesus Christ, to become like Jesus Christ, to be useful to Jesus Christ, the return of Jesus Christ, and the blessing in this life and the life to come from Jesus Christ our Lord.

    d. This leads to further obedience to God. We will see things such as humility, patience, peace, joy, self-sacrifice, kindness, goodness, mercy, love, faith, gentleness, self-control, and wisdom. This leads to a peaceful conscience, a confidence in the presence of God, and a desire to draw near to God resulting in drawing near to God. (Galatians 5:22-25)

Illustration of Point III

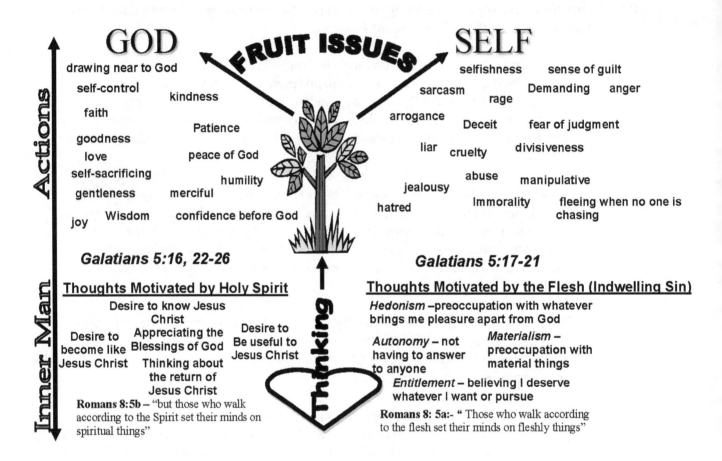

GOD

drawing near to God

self-control   kindness

faith

    Patience

goodness

love   peace of God

self-sacrificing

    humility

gentleness   merciful

joy   Wisdom   confidence before God

FRUIT ISSUES

SELF

selfishness   sense of guilt

sarcasm   rage   Demanding   anger

arrogance   Deceit   fear of judgment

liar   cruelty   divisiveness

jealousy   abuse   manipulative

hatred   Immorality   fleeing when no one is chasing

Actions

Galatians 5:16, 22-26

Galatians 5:17-21

Inner Man

Thoughts Motivated by Holy Spirit

Desire to know Jesus Christ

Desire to become like Jesus Christ

Appreciating the Blessings of God

Thinking about the return of Jesus Christ

Desire to Be useful to Jesus Christ

Romans 8:5b – "but those who walk according to the Spirit set their minds on spiritual things"

Thinking

Thoughts Motivated by the Flesh (Indwelling Sin)

Hedonism –preoccupation with whatever brings me pleasure apart from God

Autonomy – not having to answer to anyone

Materialism – preoccupation with material things

Entitlement – believing I deserve whatever I want or pursue

Romans 8: 5a:- " Those who walk according to the flesh set their minds on fleshly things"

Graphics by Cathy Poulos

The Point of Choice

IV. **When our thoughts are driven by the flesh (sin in our hearts) we will begin to worship our desires, turning them into the lusts of our lives.** *(James 4:1-3) (See Illustration of Point IV and V)*

    a. Our minds will be set on things below instead of things above leading us to make self interest a priority over God's will. We focus less and less on loving God and loving others; we focus more and more on using God and using others according to our self interest. (Philippians 3:17-19, James 3:13-4:3)

    b. Our desires will become preoccupations resulting in us looking for avenues to satisfy these desires we have started to worship. We look to any person, place, product, or perspective we believe will satisfy these desires we have started to worship above loving God and loving others. (James 4:1-3)

    c. We will build our lives around these desires we have started to worship above loving God and loving others.
(Philippians 3:17-19)

    d. We will become servants of our flesh to satisfy these desires we have started to worship above loving God and loving others. (Galatians 5:16-21)

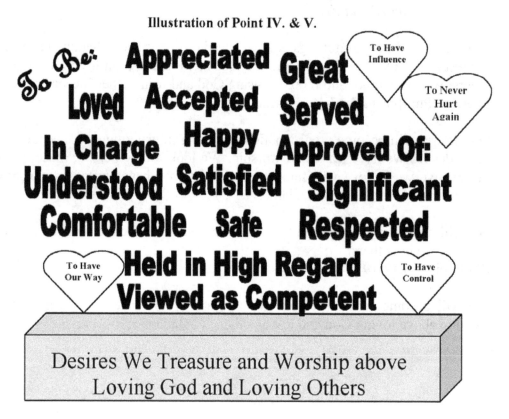

Graphics by Audra Anderson

The Point of Choice

V. **As we make choices according to the desires we have begun to worship we will find ourselves on a path of difficulty and hard times.** *(Proverbs 13:15) (See Illustration of Point IV and V)*

a. We will become a slave to that which we pursue above loving God and loving others. (2Peter 2:18-19)

b. We will develop sinful habits that are hard to repent and replace as a result pursing those desires we worship above loving God and loving others. (Proverbs 5:21-22)

c. We will reap negative consequences of our sinful habits and pursuit of those desires we worship above loving God and loving others. (Galatians 6:7-8)

d. We will have a negative effect on the lives of those around us as a result of pursuing those desires we worship above loving God and loving others. (1Corinthians 5:1-6)

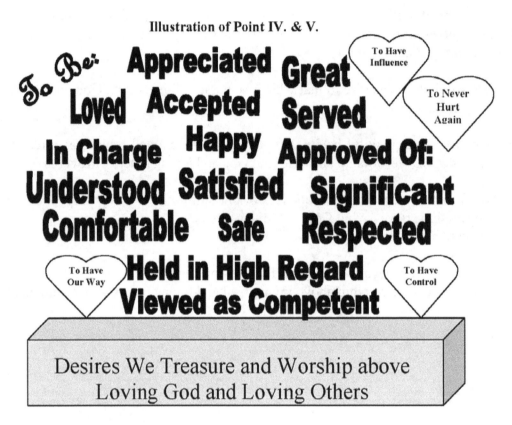

Graphics by Audra Anderson

The Point of Choice

VI. **We must turn from a self-centered life to a God-Centered life through the Person, Power and Precepts of Jesus Christ.** *(Romans 13:8-14)(See Illustration of Point VI)*

    a. We must identify the areas of our lives where we are dominated by lies, selfish ambition, hedonism, autonomy, materialism, entitlement, and lustful pursuits above loving God and loving others; We must identify where this is happening in our attitudes, intentions, desires words, actions, relationship patterns and service to God and confess and repent of these things accordingly. (Proverbs 28:13-14)

    b. We must decide to make God a priority in all that we think, say and do. (1Corinthians 10:31)

    c. The areas of lives where we are dominated by lies, selfish ambition, hedonism, autonomy, materialism, entitlement, and lustful pursuits, must be replaced with specific obedience to God accordingly in those areas. (Ephesians 4:17-32, Colossians 3:1-25)

    d. In other words, we must guard our hearts from self-centeredness by walking in genuine love for God and love for others in our attitudes, intentions, desires, words, actions, relationship patterns, and service.

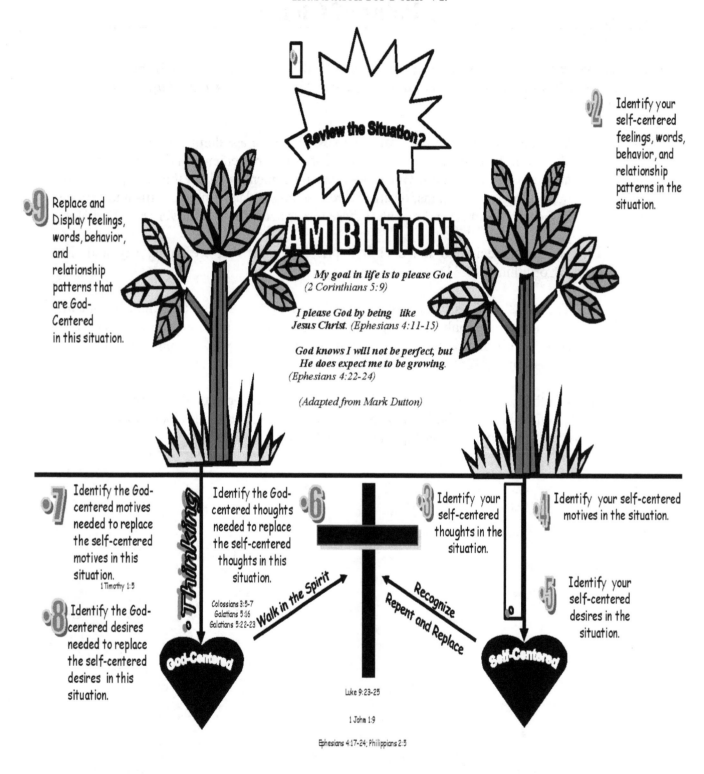

Review the Situation?

AMBITION

My goal in life is to please God.
(2 Corinthians 5:9)

I please God by being like
Jesus Christ. (Ephesians 4:11-15)

God knows I will not be perfect, but
He does expect me to be growing.
(Ephesians 4:22-24)

(Adapted from Mark Dutton)

2. Identify your self-centered feelings, words, behavior, and relationship patterns in the situation.

9. Replace and Display feelings, words, behavior, and relationship patterns that are God-Centered in this situation.

7. Identify the God-centered motives needed to replace the self-centered motives in this situation.
1 Timothy 1:5

8. Identify the God-centered desires needed to replace the self-centered desires in this situation.

Thinking

6. Identify the God-centered thoughts needed to replace the self-centered thoughts in this situation.

Colossians 3:5-7
Galatians 5:16
Galatians 5:22-23

Walk in the Spirit

God-Centered

3. Identify your self-centered thoughts in the situation.

4. Identify your self-centered motives in the situation.

5. Identify your self-centered desires in the situation.

Recognize
Repent and Replace

Self-Centered

Luke 9:23-25

1 John 1:9

Ephesians 4:17-24; Philippians 2:5

Adapted from curriculum presented in BC590s: Counseling Practicum, Dr. John Street professor, The Master's College, Santa Clarita, CA July 2004.
Graphics by Cathy Poulos

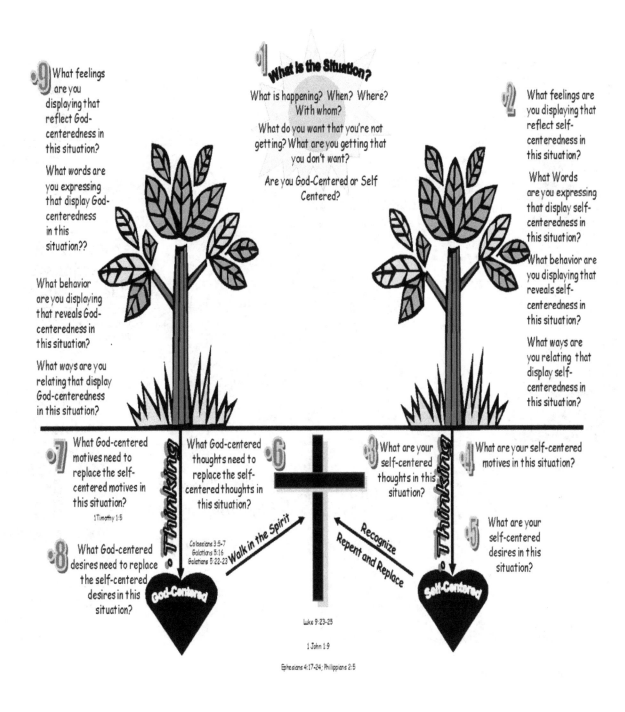

9 What feelings are you displaying that reflect God-centeredness in this situation?

What words are you expressing that display God-centeredness in this situation??

What behavior are you displaying that reveals God-centeredness in this situation?

What ways are you relating that display God-centeredness in this situation?

1 What is the Situation?

What is happening? When? Where? With whom?

What do you want that you're not getting? What are you getting that you don't want?

Are you God-Centered or Self Centered?

2 What feelings are you displaying that reflect self-centeredness in this situation?

What Words are you expressing that display self-centeredness in this situation?

What behavior are you displaying that reveals self-centeredness in this situation?

What ways are you relating that display self-centeredness in this situation?

7 What God-centered motives need to replace the self-centered motives in this situation?
1 Timothy 1:5

What God-centered thoughts need to replace the self-centered thoughts in this situation?

Thinking

6

3 What are your self-centered thoughts in this situation?

4 What are your self-centered motives in this situation?

Thinking

8 What God-centered desires need to replace the self-centered desires in this situation?

God-Centered

Colossians 3:5-7
Galatians 5:16
Galatians 5:22-23

Walk in the Spirit

Recognize Repent and Replace

5 What are your self-centered desires in this situation?

Self-Centered

Luke 9:23-25

1 John 1:9

Ephesians 4:17-24; Philippians 2:5

Graphics by Cathy Poulos

Illustration for point VI.

Graphics by Adrian Baxter

Discussion Questions

1. When looking at the choices that you have made today, were you self-centered or God centered in your choices? Write down you findings. .

   _____
   _____
   _____
   _____
   _____

2. Identify thought patterns you have which are rooted in lies and selfish ambition then identify thought patterns you have that are rooted in truth and godly wisdom. Explain how these thought patterns determined your choices above.

   _____
   _____
   _____
   _____

3. What desires have you allowed becoming a form of worship resulting in further complications in your life?

   _____
   _____
   _____
   _____
   _____

4. What loving thoughts, motives, desires words, actions, relationship patterns and service do you need to walk in to replace the sin you are in?

   _____
   _____
   _____
   _____
   _____

Section Three

Idolatrous Lust

Understanding Idolatry

I. **The *Characteristics* of Idolatry: (Jeremiah 2:13)**

    A. Idolatry is depending on some aspect of life or creation as you should depend on God which in Jeremiah was categorized as broken cisterns. Broken cisterns are man-made unreliable large pits dug in the rock covered with plaster used to gather rainwater. When cracks developed in the cisterns, they would hold no water unlike the reliable natural springs of living water which always provided water no matter the situation which was symbolizing God. (Bible Knowledge Commentary /The Book of Jeremiah)

    B. Idolatry is dependence of some aspect of life creation at the level of worship above God to get what we treasure above God.

    C. Idolatry is the dependence on certain aspects of life or creation at the level of worship above God making them the avenue to of our satisfaction and solutions to our problems.

    D. Idolatry is the preoccupation with some aspect of life or creation above and apart from the Creator to bring some longing(s) of our hearts that have become the lusts of our hearts.

II. **The *Creation* of Idolatry: (Jeremiah 2:13)**

    A. Idols are created when we no longer look to God as the source of our satisfaction.

    B. Idols are created when we no longer look to God as the solution to our problems.

    C. When we no longer look to God as the source of our satisfaction, we look to His creation to bring it us.

    D. When we no longer to look to God as the solution to our problems, we look to His creation to bring it to us.

III. **The *Criticism* and *Consequences* of Idolatry: (Jeremiah 2:13, Ezekiel 14:3)**

    A. Idolatry is evil in the sight of God.

    B. Idolatry leads you away from serving God to serving His creation.

    C. Idolatry leads you to stumbling into further sin.

    D. Idolatry leads God to address you according to your sin of Idolatry instead of the request you bring to Him.

IV. **The _Categories_ of Idolatry: Remember,** Idolatry is the dependence on certain aspects of life or creation at the level of worship above God, making them the avenue to of our satisfaction and solutions t our problems. Idolatry is the preoccupation with some aspect of life or creation above and apart from the Creator to bring some longing(s) of our hearts that have become the lusts of our hearts. **Idolatry** could be:

A. ***Depending on People as the source to our satisfaction and the solution to our problems*** above and apart from God to bring some longing(s) of our hearts that have become the lust(s) of our hearts making the lust(s) the source of our satisfaction and the end our problems.

B. ***Depending on Places as the source to our satisfaction and the solution to our problems*** above and apart from God to bring some longing(s) of our hearts that have become the lust(s) of our hearts making the lust(s) the source of our satisfaction and the end of our problems.

C. ***Depending on Products as the source to our satisfaction and the solution to our problems*** above and apart from God to bring some longing(s) of our hearts that have become the lust(s) of our hearts making the lust(s) the source of our satisfaction and the end of our problems.

D. ***Depending on Perspectives as the source to our satisfaction and the solution to our problems*** above and apart from God to bring some longing(s) of our hearts that have become the lust(s) of our hearts making the lust(s) the source of our satisfaction and the end of our problems.

E. ***Depending on Positions as the source to our satisfaction and the solution to our problems*** above and apart from God to bring some longing(s) of our hearts that have become the lust(s) of our hearts making the lust(s) the source of our satisfaction and the end of our problems.

F. ***Depending on Power as the source to our satisfaction and the solution to our problems*** above and apart from God to bring some longing(s) of our hearts that have become the lust(s) of our hearts making the lust(s) the source of our satisfaction and the end of our problems.

G. ***Depending on Platforms of influence as the source to our satisfaction and the solution to our problems above*** and apart from God to bring some longing(s) of our hearts that have become the lust(s) of our hearts making the lust(s) the source of our satisfaction and the end of our problems.

H. ***Depending on Politics as the source to our satisfaction and the solution to our problems*** above and apart from God to bring some longing(s) of our hearts that have become the lust(s) of our hearts making the lust(s) the source of our satisfaction and the end of our problems.

I. ***Depending on Money as the source to our satisfaction and the solution to our problems*** above and apart from God to bring some longing(s) of our hearts that have become the lust(s) of our hearts making the lust(s) the source of our satisfaction and the end of our problems.

J. ***Depending on Medication as the source to our satisfaction and the solution to our problems*** above and apart from God to bring some longing(s) of our hearts that have become the lust(s) of our hearts making the lust(s) the source of our satisfaction and the end of our problems.

K. ***Depending on Media as the source to our satisfaction and the solution to our problems*** above and apart from God to bring some longing(s) of our hearts that have become the lust(s) of our hearts making the lust(s) the source of our satisfaction and the end of our problems.

L. ***Depending on Ministry as the source to our satisfaction and the solution to our problems*** above and apart from God to bring some longing(s) of our hearts that have become the lust(s) of our hearts making the lust(s) the source of our satisfaction and the end of our problems.

The Discipline
We can expect God to address our sin of idolatry as He sees fit while not addressing our prayer request as we desire.
If we keep resisting God's discipline we fall further away from God resulting in further negative consequences to experience as a result.

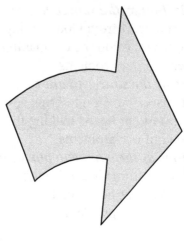

The Dilemma
We no longer accept and embrace God as the source of our satisfaction and the solution to our problems.

Cycle of Idolatry

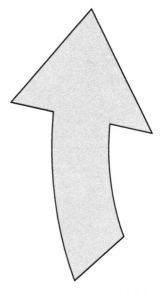

The Direction
When God is no longer the source of our satisfaction and the solution to our problems we make man and creation big and God small resulting in a lack of fellowship with God leading to deeper sin in our lives.

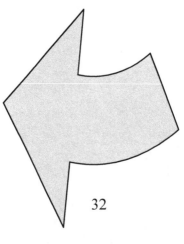

The Downfall
We turn from God and turn to His creation as the source to our satisfaction and the solution to our problems.

Understanding Lust

I. The Characteristics of the Lusts of Our Hearts: (James 1:13-14)

A. Lusts of the hearts are longings that have become constant cravings of our hearts in an evil or wrong way.

B. Lusts of the hearts are longings that have moved from something we want to something we must have making something that was once a good thing now an evil thing; making it a sin in our lives because we are consumed with it above God and His will.

C. Lusts of the hearts are longings that have become such a preoccupation of our hearts that we are easily enticed by the devil when it comes to them because they have become inordinate, sinful affections of our soul.

D. Lusts of the hearts are longings that have become such a preoccupation of our hearts that we are willing to sin to obtain them, sin to keep them, sin when do not receive them, or sin when we lose them making those longings a worship in our lives above worship and obedience to God.

II. The Commitment to the Lusts of Our Hearts: (Ezekiel 33:31)

A. When we are committed to the lusts of our hearts, we will still listen to truth and delight in the truth we hear, but we will not obey that truth because we are preoccupied with the lusts of our hearts.

B. When we are committed to the lusts of our hearts, they become a constant topic of discussion.

C. When we are committed to the lusts of our hearts we are in constant pursuit of obtaining them.

D. When we are committed to the lusts of our hearts, we do not find obedience to God something to be treasured above those lusts we have treasured in our hearts.

III. The Cancer of the Lusts of Our Hearts: (James 4:1-4)

A. The lusts of our hearts can lead us to kill others or at least be envious of them.

B. The lusts of our hearts can lead us to create conflict with others.

C. The lusts of our hearts can lead us to pray selfishly.

D. The lusts of our hearts can lead us to be friends with the world's system resulting in acting as enemies of God.

IV. **The Consequences of the Lusts of Our Hearts: (James 1:15, Galatians 6:7-8)**

A. The lusts of our hearts lead to walking in further sin in our thoughts, words, or actions.
B. Walking in further sin in our thoughts, words, or actions reveals that one is walking in the flesh which leads to corruption in one's life which ultimately leads to death.
C. This could be physical death where as a result of a Christian's unrepentant sin one is now disciplined by God by being taken from earth to be with Him resulting is lost rewards for eternity as a result of constant disobedience on earth. (1Corinthains 11:23-32)
D. This could be eternal death where as a result of an unbeliever's life of sin he/she now faces the consequences of rejecting God and living a life of sin which is burning in hell forever. (Revelation 20:11-15)

V. **The Categories of The Lusts of Our Hearts: Remember, *Lusts* of our hearts are** desires we believe we cannot do without being satisfied; We are willing to sin to obtain them, sin to keep them, sin when do not receive them, or sin when we lose them making those longings a worship in our lives above worship and obedience to God. It could be a desire:

A. *To be loved* by others that have become a demand or a craving we believe we can't live without.
B. *To be accepted* by others that has become a demand or a craving we believe we can't live without.
C. *To be understood* by others that has become a demand or a craving we believe we can't live without.
D. *To never be hurt or disappointed* by others that has become a demand or a craving we believe we can't live without.
E. *To be respected by others* that have become a demand or a craving we believe we can't live without.
F. *To be served by others* that have become a demand or a craving we believe we can't live without.
G. *To have personal preferences accommodated at all times* that has become a demand or a craving we believe we can't live without.
H. *To be viewed as competent by others* that has become a demand or a craving we believe we can't live without.
I. *To be approved of by others* that have become a demand or a craving we believe we can't live without.
J. *To belong to someone* that has become a demand or a craving we believe we can't live without.
K. *To be held in high regard by others* that have become a demand or a craving we believe we can't live without.
L. *To be significant to others* that have become a demand or a craving we believe we can't live without.

M. *To be satisfied by others* that has become a demand or a craving we believe we can't live without.
N. *To maintain a favorable position with others* that has become a demand or a craving we believe we can't live without.
O. *To be secure/ safe with others* that have become a demand or a craving we believe we can't live without.
P. *To never be alone* that has become a demand or a craving we believe we can't live without.
Q. *To have someone exposed for the way they have mistreated* us that has become a demand or a craving we believe we can't live without.
R. *To have someone to suffer the consequences for what they did to us* that has become a demand or a craving we believe you can't live without.

On the next page is "The Cycle of Lust":

The Display of Disobedience

If we do not resist the temptation to find our delight in this world instead of in Jesus Christ we will walk in a lack of love for God and a lack of love for others revealing a life that is consumed with

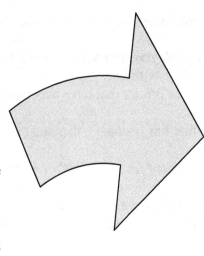

The Dialogue of the World

Satan uses the world to speak to the desires of our hearts that have become the lusts of our hearts

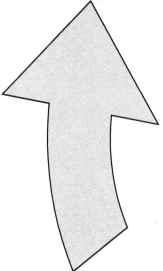

The Direction of our Lives

If we do not resist the temptation to find our delight in the world instead of in Jesus Christ, we will live by earthly, natural, demonic wisdom, the lust of the flesh, the lust of the eyes and the

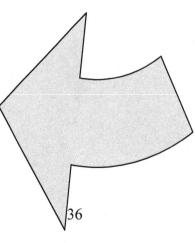

The Deliberation of Our Hearts

As the world speaks to our hearts appealing to the lusts of our hearts while presenting various delights in the world that will lead us into sin to obtain or maintain the lusts of our hearts, our minds contemplate pursuing or resisting

Idolatrous Lust

Definition of Idolatrous Lust: *Something you bow down to that you believe will bring you what you truly treasure while making what you truly treasure something you bow down to in place of the living God. It is the various aspects of life and creation we worship above the Creator as well as the basic ways we worship the creation above the Creator. Romans 1:18-32*

I. **The *avenues* we pursue and bow down to in the form of worship (Idols) along with these treasures we bow down to in the form of worship (Lusts) make up the idolatrous lust in our lives. (Romans 1:18-25) Examples:**

    A. Bowing down to ***people*** (***Idol***) as we should God to receive the ***acceptance*** we treasure and crave in an inordinate way (***Lust***) in place of loving God and loving others is ***idolatrous lust***.

    B. Bowing down to ***education*** (***Idol***) as we should God in order to be ***viewed as competent*** which we treasure and crave in an inordinate way (***Lust***) in place of loving God and loving others is ***idolatrous lust***.

    C. Bowing down to ***money*** (***Idol***) as we should God to receive the comfort we treasure and crave in an inordinate way (***Lust***) in place of loving God and loving others is ***idolatrous lust***.

    D. Bowing down to ***control*** (***Idol***) as we should God to receive the ***security*** we treasure and crave in an inordinate way (***Lust***) in place of loving God and loving others is ***idolatrous lust***.

II. **There is a process by which we are lead into *Idolatrous Lust*:**

    A. *Mindset*: Your mind is set on things below instead of things above. (Philippians 3:17-19)

    B. *Motivation*: You begin to make self- interest a priority above God's will. (James 3:13-4:3)

    C. *Meditation*: Your desires become preoccupations resulting in becoming lust. (James 4:1-3)

    D. *Methods:* You look for avenues to satisfy your desires which have now become lust.

    E. *Manner*: You bow down and submit to these avenues in order to obtain what you have turned into lust thus making these avenues idols you bow down to in order to get what you lust after. (Philippians 3:17-19)

F. *Mastered*: You become a servant of your flesh (Galatians 5:16-21)

III.   How Do You Repent of Idolatrous Lusts? (Proverbs 28:13-14)

A. Identify desires or cravings that have preoccupied your minds to the point of lust.

B. Identify the avenues you have pursed and thus have bowed down to in the place of God to obtain these desires or cravings that have preoccupied your minds to the point of lust.

C. Identify the sinful thoughts, attitudes, and behaviors that have come about as a result of these desires or cravings that have preoccupied your minds to the point of lust.

D. Confess the lusts, idols, sinful thoughts, sinful attitudes, and sinful behaviors you have identified, to God and others accordingly.

E. Replace your lusts, idols, sinful thoughts, sinful attitudes, and sinful behaviors you have identified, with genuine worship of God, and godly thoughts, godly attitudes, and godly behaviors.

F. Decide to make God priority over all and everything.

G. Guard your heart.

Examining the Heart Journal

1. What did you want today or what were you expecting to happen today?

_____

_____

_____

2. Who did you want it from or expect it to come from?

_____

_____

_____

3. What desire(s) would this fulfill in your life?

_____

_____

_____

4. How much of your time was spent thinking, speaking, and acting on what you wanted?

_____

_____

_____

5. What ways did you sin in thoughts, words, or actions to get what you wanted?

_____

_____

_____

6. What ways did you sin in thoughts, words, or actions when you did not get what you wanted?

_____

_____

_____

7. What person(s) did you sin against to get what you wanted?

_____

_____

_____

8. What person(s) did you sin against because you did not get what you wanted?

_____

_____

_____

9. What were your attitudes and actions like towards God and others as a result getting what you wanted today?

_____
_____
_____

10. What were your attitudes and actions like towards God and others as a result of not getting what you wanted today?

_____
_____
_____

11. What biblical standards or principles could you use to explain your thoughts, words, and actions today?

_____
_____
_____

12. What biblical standards or principles should you have practiced in thoughts, words, or actions today?

_____
_____
_____

13. Were you thoughts, words, and actions towards others based primarily on how you felt or what God commanded? Explain

_____
_____
_____

Section Four

Understanding Worry

I. The *Content* of Worry (Psalm 139:23) David asks God to reveal David's *anxious* thoughts. In the context of this passage *anxious* means worry. To know what God would reveal in David we need to know what worry is.

   A. Worry can be defined as disturbing or disquieting thoughts of the mind due to preoccupation with the possibility of not getting something you want or need that is very important to you from this world below and in this world below.

   B. Worry can defined as disturbing or disquieting thoughts of the mind due to preoccupation with the possibility of losing something you want or need that is very important to you from this world below and in this world below.

   C. Worry can defined as disturbing or disquieting thoughts of the mind due to preoccupation with the possibility of getting something you do not want or need that is important to you from this world below and in this world below.

   D. In essence, worry is the fear of not getting something you want or need, the fear losing something you want or need, or the fear of getting something you don't want or need as a result of being consumed and controlled by these things that are very important to you from this world below and in this world below.

II. The *Cause* of Worry (Luke 10:38-42): Jesus *challenged* Martha about her worry. Martha exposes to us what causes worry.

   A. Worry is caused by reducing life to what you want and what you think you need from this world below and in this world below resulting in the fear of not getting something you want or need, the fear losing something you want or need, or the fear of getting something you don't want or need from this world below (intangible) and in this world below (tangible).

   B. Worry is caused by trying to control the good and bad that God controls in your life, instead of enjoying and enduring what God ordains in your life. This results in the fear of not getting something you want or need, the fear of losing something you want or need, or the fear of getting something you don't want or need from this world below and in this world below.

C. Worry is caused by trusting one's own knowledge or past experience and evaluating things according to that knowledge or past experience without considering or acting on God's Word; This results in the fear of not getting something you want or need, the fear of losing something you want or need, or the fear of getting something you don't want or need from this world below and in this world below.

D. In essence, worry is caused by one's interpretation of a situation apart from trusting God's sovereignty, sufficiency, or wisdom resulting in preoccupation with your own cares, own riches, personal standards or past experiences.

III. **The _Characteristics_ of Worry (Proverbs 12:25): Worry can create a heavy burden in one's _heart._ When something has become a heavy burden in your life it _controls_ and _consumes_ you. For example:**

A. Sometimes when you worry, you are controlled and consumed with the outcome of situations/circumstances causing your heart to be loaded down with this burden.

B. Sometimes when you worry, you are controlled and consumed with the responses and reactions of people causing your heart to be loaded down with this burden.

C. Sometimes when you worry, you are controlled and consumed with the loosing or gaining of the needs or wants of life causing your heart to be loaded down with this burden.

D. In essence, when you worry, you are controlled and consumed with things you can't keep from happening or things you can't cause to happen resulting in your heart being loaded down with this burden. (This can lead to irresponsibility in the things you can control.)

IV. **The _Counteractions_ to Worry**

A. Identify the fears that have consumed your time.

B. Identify the desires behind the fears (behind every fear there is a desire for (something ex. Fear of rejection = Desire for approval).

C. Identify the people, places, things, and situations you believe are the source and the solution to your needs, desires, and problems.

D. Confess and repent of trying to control the uncontrollable (Job 38-42, Proverbs 28:13-14).

E. Confess and repent of making people, places, and outcome of events idols of your Heart (Ezekiel 14:1-11).

F. Confess and repent of making desires of your heart lusts in your life (James 1:13-14, 4:1-3).

G. Study, learn and accept the sovereignty of God in all things (Ecclesiastes 3:1-11, 7:13-14, 9:1, 11:5, Colossians 1:15-17).

H. Making the most of your time by focusing on your God-given roles and responsibilities within your condition and circumstances (Romans 12:3-8, 1Peter 4:10).

I. Give thanks for your condition and circumstances knowing God will use it to bring about His glory and our good through our condition and circumstances (Romans 8:28, 1Thessalonians 5:18).

J. You must accept God's redemptive agenda in the matter and embrace it accordingly knowing that whatever happens will work out to your progressive sanctification (Romans 8:28-29).

Section Five

The Fear of Man
(Proverbs 29:25)

I.   **What is the Fear of Man?**

    A.   To be afraid of man.

    B.   To respect man as God.

    C.   To depend on man as source of life.

II.   **What Do We Fear of Man?**

    A.   We fear being exposed (John 3:19-21).

    B.   We fear being rejected (John 12:42-43).

    C.   We fear being physically hurt or oppressed (Genesis 12:11-13).

    D.   We fear being denied what we desire (John 12:42-43).

III.   **Why Do We Fear Man?**

    A.   We lack genuine love for God and others (John 14:21,1John 4:18-21).

    B.   We believe man is the means to satisfy our needs and desires (Jeremiah 17:5-6, Js. 4:1-3).

    C.   We believe man is the source to solving or creating our problems (Proverbs 29:26).

    D.   We are preoccupied with what man can do to us above what God can do to us (Matthew10:28-31).

IV.   **Implications of the Fear of Man**

    A.   To the extent one believes that man's thoughts, behaviors, and actions are the source or solution to their needs, desires, and problems is the extent they may seek to bow down or suck up to man to obtain what their desire or to keep from losing what they currently have (John 12:42-43, Proverbs 29:25-26, Romans 1:18-25).

    B.   To the extent one believes that man's thoughts, behaviors, and actions are the source or solution to their needs, desires and problems is the extent they may try to deceive or lie to man to obtain what they desire or to keep from losing what they have (1Sammuel 15:1-35).

C. To the extent one believes that man's thoughts, behaviors, and actions are the source or solution to their needs, desires and problems is the extent one may try to control or manipulate man to obtain what they desire or to keep from losing what they have (Esther 3:1-7:10).

V. Questions we must Consider

A. What is it that you need?
B. Who do you believe is responsible for supplying that need?
C. Who are you depending on to meet that need?
D. What actions do you take to meet that need?
E. How do you respond when your need goes unmet?
F. Is what you calling a need truly a need or is it a desire you have elevated to a demand which you have made a need?
G. Can you love God and love your neighbor without it?
H. Is it something that the Bible would validate as a need?
I. Is it something that keeps you bound to the thoughts, behaviors, and actions of man in order to have it?
J. Is it possible that you have elevated a desire to a demand which has turned into a lust which now feels like a need?

VI. Desires we elevate to demands which turn into lusts which feel like needs that lead us into the Fear of Man

A. To be in control
B. To be loved
C. To be accepted
D. To be understood
E. To never be hurt or disappointed
F. To be respected
G. To be served
H. To have personal preferences accommodated at all times
I. To be viewed as competent
J. To be approved of
K. To belong to someone
L. To be held in high regard
M. To be significant
N. To be fulfilled
O. To be satisfied
P. To be valuable to others
Q. To maintain a favorable position with others
R. To be secure/safe
S. To never be alone

VII. How Do We Overcome the Fear of Man?

A. Identify the fears that have consumed your time.

B. Identify the desires behind the fears (behind every fear there is a desire for (something ex. Fear of rejection = Desire for approval).

C. Identify the people, places, things, and situations you believe are the source and the solution to your needs, desires, and problems.

D. Examine the Scripture to see if your belief in C lines up with what the Scripture says you need to love God and to love others (Luke 10:38-42,Timothy 6:6-8, Matthew 4:1-11).

E. Confess and repent of trying to control the uncontrollable (Job 38-42, Proverbs 28:13-14)

F. Confess and repent of making people, places, and outcome of events idols of your Heart (Ezekiel 14:1-11).

G. Minimize your focus on what people think of you (1Corinthians 4:3).

H. Maximize your focus on what God thinks of you (1Corinthians 4:4).

I. Study, learn and accept the sovereignty of God in all things (Ecclesiastes 3:1-11, 7:13-14, 9:1, 11:5, Colossians 1:15-17).

J. Accept the fact that you will have to give an account of your life to God not people (1Corinthians 4:5, Romans 14:10-12, 2 Corinthians 5:10, Ecclesiastes 12:13-14).

K. Accept that fact that every good and perfect gift is from God not man (James 1:16-17).

L. Accept the fact all that you need comes from God not man (2Peter 1:1-3, Philippians 4:19, Romans 8:31-32, Psalm 145:8-16, Hebrews 4:16).

M. Look to God for justice and not man (Proverbs 29:26, Romans 12:19).

N. Don't insist that people live a life to please you; insist they live a life to please God (Galatians 1:10, 1Corinthians 10:31).

O. Humble yourself and submit to the doctrines/disciplines/duties of the Christian faith (2Peter 1:1-10, 1Peter 4:10, Romans 12:1-21, 2 John).

P. Practice serving people according to God's Will and not according to how you feel or what you want from them in return 1Corinthians 13:1-8, Romans 12:9- 21, John 13:34-35, Luke 6:31-38)

Q. Practice setting your mind on God's agenda in every aspect of your life and seek to live according to that agenda (Matthew 6:33, Colossians 3:1-25, Ephesians 5:1-18).

The Fear of Man Check List

(Place a Check by the things you see yourself doing.)

_____ Peer pressure

_____ Difficulty saying no to others.

_____ Consumed with what you perceive you need from others.

_____ Consumed with what you don't want from others.

_____ Justifying your mistakes to others.

_____ Second guessing decisions because of what others may think.

_____ Getting embarrassed.

_____ Telling lies to cover up.

_____ Anger (not getting what you want or getting what you don't want).

_____ Preoccupation with how you look.

_____ Avoiding or isolating self from others.

_____ Feeling good or bad about yourself according to the standards of people around you.

_____ Constantly comparing yourself to others.

_____ Avoiding sharing your faith.

_____ Compromising your beliefs because of the setting you are in.

_____ Feeling controlled by the thoughts, behaviors, and actions of others.

_____ Spending a lot of time focusing on what others can or will do to you.

_____ Spending a lot of time focusing on what others will not do for you.

_____ Spending a lot of time focusing on what others can or will do for you.

_____ Constantly trying to measure up to standards set by people.

_____ Talking in terms of what you need from others instead of what you desire.

_____ Cannot be happy or content unless certain people in your life are "meeting your need" or satisfying personal preferences.

_____ Constantly trying to protect yourself from what people can say or do to you.

_____ You can remember more about your embarrassments than your sin.

_____ You can remember more about being offended, rejected, or denied than you can offending, rejecting and denying Jesus Christ.

_____ Trying to say what you think will please or provoke others to get what you want.

_____ Worry whether people like you or not.

_____ Wanting to do things for yourself and by yourself so that people will not bother You.

(Check list derived from insights in the book When People are Big and God is Small by Ed T. Welch.)

Section Six

Understanding Anger

I. The *Definition* of Anger (Ephesians 4:26-32)

    A. Disposition of the mind that entertains antagonism towards another individual, manifesting itself in various emotions and actions. (Genesis 4:1-8, Mark 3:1-6)

    B. Anger is an attitude that results in emotions that move into action. (Proverbs. 14:17,29,15:18,16:32,19:19,22:24-25)

    C. Anger can be godly/righteous indignation- To be troubled or disgusted in attitude or action as a result of someone disgracing God or disregarding His Holy Laws. (Exodus 32:1-30, Ephesians 4: 26-27, John 2:12-17, Nehemiah 5:1-13)

    D. Anger can be worldly/sinful of man- to have ungodly attitudes and actions as a result of some perceived need, desire, personal preference /standard not being met by someone or being offended by someone. (Numbers 20:1-13, Ephesians 4:31-32, I Samuel 18:6-8, 20:24-34; James 1:19-20, Matthew 5:21-22)

II. The *Deliberation* on Righteous Indignation Vs. Worldly/Sinful Anger of Man (Ephesians 4:26-32)

    A. Godly Anger or Righteous Indignation is the exception to the rule; Very seldom when one is angry it is about the things that disgrace God or disregard His Holy Laws. When one is walking in righteous indignation he/she is filled with desire to see justice done for the glory of God(not self) as he/she is walking by the Spirit of God in this kind of anger. When one does act in Godly anger or righteous indignation he/she is commanded to deal with it before the day is over so that the devil does not use it against him/her to lead him/her into sin.

    B. Generally, when people are angry it has nothing to do with someone disgracing God or disregarding His Holy Laws; They are not thinking about God, His holy laws, His righteousness, His will or His ways; They are thinking about themselves, their feelings, their wants, or their needs. They are self-centered not God-centered. They are preoccupied with what they crave, the means to the end that is not providing that craving or something that is hindering that craving from being realized.

    C. Therefore, most of the time when people are angry it is generally worldly/ sinful anger of man; What they want within the situation is not granted; They are receiving something they do not want or they are not receiving what they want.

D. As a result of not receiving what they want or getting what they don't want, ungodly attitudes and actions begin to manifest; Instead of being thankful to God for how he will use the situation or accepting what God has allowed in the situation they become negative and ungodly in thoughts, words, actions, and relational patterns.

III. The *Details* of Life that Can lead to Worldly/Sinful Anger of Man

A. Worldly/ sinful anger of man may occur as a result of misplaced dependency- depending on people, place, things, or events to provide what only God provides.

B. Worldly/ sinful anger of man may occur as a result of unrealistic expectations- expecting things that are beyond the scope of possibility.

C. Worldly/sinful anger of man may occur as a result of being untrained in handling disappointments- not accepting the fallibility of people, places, things and events.

D. Worldly/sinful anger of man may occur as a result of not accepting powerlessness over people, places, outcomes of events- resisting the fact that you were not designed to control people and outcome of events.

IV. The *Desires* that become *Demands* of the Heart which is the source of Worldly/Sinful Anger of Man (James 4:1-2)

A. When the desire to be affirmed becomes a demand to be affirmed, worldly/sinful anger of man
results when your demands are not met.

B. When the desire to not be put down by others becomes a demand not to be put down by others, worldly/sinful anger of man results when your demands are not met.

C. When the desires that are centered on things of this life become a demand for things of this life, worldly/ sinful anger of man results when your demands are not met:
   1. You walk in worldly/sinful anger of man when you demand_____ and do not get it:

      ➤ To have control ,To be loved, To be accepted, To be understood
      ➤ To never hurt again, To be respected, To be served, To have your way
      ➤ To be viewed as competent, To be approved of, To belong to someone
      ➤ To be held in high regard, To maintain a favorable position with people

D. When the desire for people to do or handle things your way or for life to go your way becomes a demand, worldly/ sinful anger of man results when your demands are not met.

V. The *Different* Expressions of Worldly/ Sinful Anger of Man (Ephesians 4:31)

A. Bitterness- resentment.

B. Wrath- intense fury or rage.

C. Anger – deep seated hostility within the heart toward another.

D. Clamor- verbal fighting with people/ Slander- ugly words, mean words in reference to someone's reputation, verbal abuse in reference to someone's character.

VI. The *Dangerous* ways people deal with anger (James 1:19-20, Ephesians 4:26-27)

A. Suppress- acting like it does not exist.
B. Aggression- openly expressed anger at someone else's expense.
C. Passive Aggressive- indirectly expressed anger at someone else's expense.
D. Do not deal with it before the day is done.

VII. The *Direction* to Deal With Anger James 1:19,Ephesians 4:31, Colossians 3:1-8)

A. Acknowledge your anger.
B. Confess the sin of your anger.
C. Identify the details of life whereby you have chosen to be angry.
D. Identify the specific desires you have been demanding to be fulfilled by God, people, places, events resulting in responding in anger as a result of not getting your way.
E. Accept your inability to control God, people, and the outcome of circumstances
F. Accept these conditions:
   1. The Person may be willing and able
   2. The Person may be willing and unable
   3. The Person may be unwilling and able
   4. The Person may be unwilling and unable
   5. It may be a desire that was not meant to be satisfied
G. Accept responsibility for your unloving thoughts, words, deeds, in the situation.
H. Repent of unloving thoughts, words, deeds in the situation.
I. Choose to serve and love others unconditionally.
J. Follow the Biblical Mandate according to the relationship. (1Cor13:4-7)
   1. Husband/Wife (Eph. 5:18-33, Col. 3:18-19, I Peter 3:1-12)
   2. Children (Eph. 6:1-2, Col. 3:20)
   3. Parent (Eph. 6:4, Col. 3:21, Deut. 6:6-9, Prov. 22:6)
   4. Friends (Prov. 27:5-6, Prov. 17:17,Prov. 27:9, Prov. 18:24)
   5. Others (I Peter 3:8-12, Rom. 12:9-21, Gal. 6:1-10)
   6. Leaders (I Tim. 4:16, Heb. 13:7, 17;I Peter 5:5, I Tim. 5:17-22, Luke 6:40)
   7. Employer/Employee (Eph. 6:5-9, I Peter 2:18-29)
   8. Government (Rom.13:1-2, I Peter 2:13-17)
   9. Enemies (Luke 6:27-36)
K. Don't allow it to go beyond that day. (Ephesians 4:26-27)

Learning to Be Content
(Philippians 4:10-14)

Definition of Contentment: Sufficient Satisfaction within the heart through the fellowship with and power of Jesus Christ apart from external circumstances and people

I. The *Picture* of Contentment Painted by the Apostle Paul (v10-v14).

    A. Paul rejoiced in the Lord when others came through for him yet his state of mind was not conditioned upon their gift (v10-v11).
    B. Paul learned to live with what he had and let it be enough for him (v12).
    C. Paul learned to live without anticipating the provision of God (v12).
    D. Paul adjusted his desires to match his condition and circumstances (v12).
    E. Paul depended on God's power from within to cultivate contentment in his condition and circumstances (v13).
    F. Paul had fellowship with God in his condition and circumstances (v13).
    G. Paul showed appreciation when others came through for him yet he did not live for or by what others may or may not do for Him (v14).

II. The Perspective of Contentment Promoted in the Scriptures.

    A. A content person is able to accept their condition (Philippians 4:11-13).
    B. A content person is able to accept their contents (Hebrews 13:5).
    C. A content person is able to endure their circumstances (2 Corinthians 12:10).
    D. A content person is depending on Christ (Hebrews 13:5).
    E. A content person is pursuing Christ-Likeness (1Timothy 6:6-8).
    F. A content person is not a complainer (Philippians 4: 11-13).
    G. A content person has an attitude of consideration (Philippians 4:11-13).

III. The *Process* to Contentment Presented in Seven Key Steps.

    A. We must accept what God allows in our condition and circumstances and make the most of it with no complaints about it (1Peter 5:6-11, Philippians 2:14-16).
    B. We must purge ourselves of the lust that drives the discontentment (2Timothy 2:22, Romans 13:14).
    C. We must accept the fact that we are passing through this world not settling down in this world (Philippians 3:20-21,1Peter 2:11).
    D. We must learn to function by our God-given roles and responsibilities within our condition and circumstances (Romans 12:3-8, 1Peter 4:10).
    E. We must no longer demand that people satisfy us but seek to help people glorify God (Matthew 5:16, Romans 15:2-3).
    F. We must give thanks for our condition and circumstances knowing God will use it to bring about His glory and our good through our condition and circumstances (Romans 8:28, 1Thessalonians 5:18).

G. We must enjoy every pleasure that God allows, endure every pain that God allows, while living from Him, through Him, and to Him in our condition and circumstances focusing on His Covenant to us. (Ecclesiastes 5:18-20, 12:13-14, 1Corinthians 13:7, Hebrews 13:5-6).

Questions to Consider this Week

1. What do I want that I cannot control getting?

_____

_____

2. What am I getting that I don't want and I can't control it?

_____

_____

3. How am I responding in attitude to this?

_____

_____

4. How am I responding in conversation to this?

_____

_____

5. How am I responding in actions to this?

_____

_____

6. How am I treating others as a result of this?

_____

_____

7. According to Scripture how would God view my attitude, conversation, actions, and relational patterns in relation to this?

_____

_____

8. What do I need to accept that God has allowed?

_____

_____

9. How do I need to obey God in this situation?

_____

_____

10. What has God promised in His Word that I can rest on in accordance to this situation?

_____

_____

11. How can I adjust my desires to match my situation?

_____

_____

Section Seven

Self-Esteem, Self-Image, Self-Love

Key Points about Self Esteem

I. Understanding the Conscience
   A. The conscience can be defined as the faculty of the immaterial heart that judges the thoughts, intentions, words, and deeds of an individual according to the standards given it by God, governing authorities, personally acquired standards (Romans 1:18-20, 32, Romans 2:14-15, Romans 13:1-5, Romans 14: 22-23).
   B. Man's conscience is an instinctual judge of his thoughts, words, and actions accusing him when he does something that is morally wrong and excusing him when he does something that is morally right (Romans 2:14-15).
   C. The conscience is a universal entity in that all have it whether believer or unbeliever (Romans 1:18-20, Romans 2:14-15, 1Timothy 3:8-9).

II. Understanding Conscience Joy and Conscience Sorrow
   A. When a person makes a choice that is morally right their conscience will produce a joy resulting in one having a satisfaction with him (Genesis 4:1-7).
   B. When a person a makes a choice that is morally wrong their conscience will produce a sorrow resulting in one having a sense of dissatisfaction with him (Genesis 4:1-7).
   C. This sense of satisfaction and dissatisfaction with oneself is where we see the concept of self-esteem coming together.

III. Definition of Positive and Negative Self Esteem
   A. Definition of Positive Self-Esteem- satisfaction with one's self, self-respect, sense of assurance (conscience joy).
   B. Definition of Negative Self-Esteem - dissatisfaction with one's self, low self-respect, sense of insecurity (conscience sorrow).
   C. They are the by-product of right and wrong choices.

IV. Positive self-esteem is a by-product of doing what is right (Genesis 4:6-7).
   A. Positive self-esteem is characterized by a clear conscience (peace) (Romans 2:14-15).
   B. Positive self-esteem is characterized by confidence from within the heart (Proverbs 28:1).
   C. When one responds in the right way to any and all types of circumstances it will produce positive self-esteem (conscience joy) which is produced at the root by the work of the conscience (1John 3:21).

V. Negative self-esteem is a by-product of living in sin (Genesis 4:6-7).

A. Negative self-esteem is characterized by a guilty conscience (Romans 2:14-15).

B. Negative self-esteem is characterized by fearfulness within the heart (Proverbs 28:1).

C. When one responds in the wrong way to any and all circumstances it will produce negative self-esteem (conscience sorrow) which is produced at root by the work of the conscience (1 Samuel 24:1-7).

VI. When an unbeliever has positive self-esteem it is the by-product of appeasing the work of the law written in his heart (Romans 2:14-15) *(Conscience Joy)*.

A. As a non-believer lines up to the dictates of his conscience it will aid in his mental soundness by delivering him from the negative effects of a sense of guilt until the Holy Spirit convicts him of his sinful condition before a Holy God.(Romans 2:15, John 16:8-11).

B. The peace the non-believer gets from lining up with his conscience is what we call conscience joy which is universally experience by believer and unbeliever (Romans 2:15, Proverb 28:1).

C. This is why positive self-esteem occurs in an unbeliever (Romans 2:14-15) (Conscience Joy).

VII. In the worst case, when an unbeliever has positive self-esteem, it is the by-product of searing or numbing his conscience to the sense of guilt and the conscience sorrow (negative self-esteem) that results (Romans 1:28-32, Ephesians 4:17-19, Romans 2:14-15, John 14:27).

A. As a non-believer sears or numbs his conscience, he no longer feels the conscience sorrow/ negative – self-esteem that results from a guilty conscience even though he is aware of his guilt before God. (Romans 1:32, Ephesians 4:17-19, 1Timohty 4:1-2)

B. The non- believer experiences joy as a result of doing something right (conscience joy/ positive self- esteem) but not sorrow that comes from wrong doing because he has numbed or seared his conscience to the feelings of guilt that bring the conscience sorrow/ negative self- esteem. He is aware of the guilt before God but is not experiencing the conscience sorrow/ negative self-esteem with the awareness. (Romans 2:14-15, Ephesians 4:17-19, Romans 1:28-32, 1Timothy 4:1-2)

C. The non -believer experiences the peace that world gives but not the sorrow that comes from wrong doing because he has numbed or seared his conscience to the feelings of guilt that bring the conscience sorrow/negative self-esteem. He is aware of the guilt before God but is not experiencing the conscience sorrow/ negative self-esteem with the awareness. (John 14:27, Ephesians 4:17-19, 1Timothy 4:1-2)

Key Points About Self Image

I. Understanding Pride (Psalm 10:3-4, Romans 8:5-7, Acts 12:21-23,Daniel 4:31-32)

A. Pride can be defined as a mind set on self with resistance to the will of God.

B. A prideful person raises his standard for thinking, speaking and behaving above God's standard.

C. A prideful person has a view of himself that is based on his opinions and ideals apart from the Truth of God's Word.

II. Understanding Humility (John 3:26-30, Romans 12:3, Romans 8:5-7)

A. Humility is a mind set on Christ with submission to the will of God.

B. Humility is embracing a view of one's self according to the standards of God not the opinions of man or his own views.

C. A humble person adjust his standards to align with will of God.

III. Definition of Self-Image

A. One's perspective of himself.

B. One's understanding of who he is and who he is not.

C. One's perspective of his role in life.

IV. If one builds his self-image on the opinions of others, the culture and personal opinions he will develop an inaccurate self-image.

A. It will lead the person to have an inaccurate assessment of themselves before God (Luke 18:9-14).

B. This person will ultimately be trusting in mankind and his own flesh to understand himself which leads him away from Truth and from God (Jeremiah 17:5-6).

C. This person will be walking in earthly, natural, demonic wisdom (James 3:13-16).

V. If one builds his self-image on what God says is true about him according to Scripture he will develop an accurate self-image.

A. It will be based on what God's Word says is true about himself (John 8:31-32).

B. This person ultimately will be trusting in Jesus Christ to explain who he is and who he is not (John 8:31-32).

C. This person will be walking in Heavenly, Spiritual, Godly wisdom (Romans 12:2-3).

Key Points About Self-Love

I. **Understanding Love**

    A. Eros—love that is based on erotic pleasure. The greater the pleasure one gets from the other person, the greater the love one has for that person; the lesser the pleasure one gets from that person the less love they have for that person; it is conditioned upon pleasure.

    B. Stergo—love that is conditioned upon the fact that we have kinship (ex. Brother, Cousin, Uncle etc.). Since we are family I treat you okay but if we were not family I would not have any dealings with you; it is conditioned upon family connection.

    C. Phileo—love that is based upon affection for the person according to some attraction to them, like interest, common goals or aspirations. The more attraction one feels, pleasure one has or common interest that is developed the more they love the other person; the less attraction one feels, the less pleasure one has with the other person or the less they have in common with the other person they lose love for the other person; it is conditioned upon attraction and common interest or pleasures.

    D. Agape—love that is based upon the power of God to seek the highest of good of others unconditionally, no strings attached. "It is concerned not with how we feel but how we act. It responds not to the attractiveness of the other person but to the condition and need of the other person. Its motivation is not the selfish desire to enjoy the other person but the selfless desire to benefit him. Essentially, it is concerned and benevolent toward others."[1]

II. **The love that God primarily commands is Agape love (Matthew 22:34-40, John 14:21)**

    A. To love God is to keep His commandments as given in His Word.

    B. To love others is to seek the highest good of others and not to cause any harm to others.

    C. God does not command us to love ourselves.

    D. Self-love is not something that has to be taught or commanded because it is something we already do on various levels.

III. **Definition of Self Love**

    A. Regard for one's self.

    B. Regard for one's own happiness.

    C. Regard for one's own advantage

---

[1]James Boyer, *For a World Like Ours: Studies in 1 Corinthians* (Grand Rapids, Michigan: Baker Book House, 1971).

IV. The Scripture implies that we already love ourselves: (Adapted from Rich Thomson's in his book The Heart of Man and The Mental Disorders)
  A. Selfish Self Love – making self the priority for life; makes self the central interest of existence (2Timohty 3-1-5).
  B. Self- Preserving Self Love – the natural tendency to take care of ourselves and preserve our material bodies (Ephesians 5:28-29)
  C. Soul Loving Self Love – one's effort to gain wisdom and live accordingly in order guard and protect one's heart (Proverb 19:8).

V. Scripture teaches that selfish self- love leads to difficulty (2Timothy3:1-2).
  A. Preoccupation with self-breeds selfishness (James 3:13-4:7).
  B. Preoccupation with self-breeds conflict with others (James 3:13-4:7).
  C. Preoccupation with self produces disorder and every evil thing (James 3:16).

VI. Scripture teaches us to deny selfish self-love (Luke 9:23-26).
  A. We are to focus on becoming like Christ in all aspects of life (Ephesians 4:11-16).
  B. We are to focus on the Kingdom agenda of God (Luke 12:13-48).
  C. We are no longer to live for ourselves but for Christ (2Corinthians 5:11-21).

The Premise of Self-Image

Even though we are not to focus on improving our self-esteem, we are called to think soberly about ourselves (Self Image).

Definition of Self Image - One's perspective of himself; one's understanding of who he is, who he is not; one's perspective of his role in life.

I. We are commanded to have a sober view of ourselves (Romans 12:3).
A. We are to have right thinking about ourselves (Romans 12:3).
B. We are to see ourselves according to God's Standard (Ephesians 2:1-22).
C. We must not view ourselves according to personal opinions (Galatians 6:3).

II. We must view ourselves as created in the image of God (Genesis 1:26-31).
A. We were created to reflect God's character (Genesis 1:26-31).
B. We were created to be relational (Genesis 2:18).
C. We were created to be worshippers of God (John 4:23-24).
D. We have been designed with intellect (Proverbs 23:7).
E. We have been designed with a will (Ecclesiastes 2:4-8).
F. We have been designed with emotions (Acts 20:36-38).

III. We must view ourselves according to our biological design (Genesis1:26-27).
A. If we were created male we must view ourselves according to our male distinctions and functions (1Corinthians 11:1-12).
B. If we were created female we must view ourselves according to our female distinctions and functions (1Corinthians 11:1-12).

IV. We must view ourselves according to our Position in Christ (2Corinthians 5:17).
A. Man in Christ is forgiven of His sin against God (1John 2:1-2).
B. Man in Christ is placed in the family of God (Ephesians 2:11-19).
C. Man in Christ is made alive from within to connect with God (Ephesians 2:1-10).
D. Man in Christ is given the Holy Spirit to empower him to live as God desires (Romans 8:12-17).
E. Man in Christ is set apart to God and made useful and pleasing to God through the power of the Holy Spirit working in him (Ephesians 2:8-10).

V. We must view ourselves according to the Biblical Roles we have been given.
A. Husband/Wife (Ephesians 5:18-33, Colossians 3:18-19, I Peter 3:1-12)
B. Son/Daughter (Ephesians 6:1-2, Col. 3:20)
C. Parent (Ephesians 6:4, Colossians 3:21, Deuteronomy 6:6-9, Proverbs 22:6)
D. Friend (Proverbs 27:5-6, Proverbs 17:17, Proverbs 27:9, Proverbs 18:24)
E. Leader (I Timothy 4:16, Hebrews 13:7, 17; I Peter 5:5, I Timothy 5:17-22, Luke 6:40)
F. Employer/Employee (Ephesians 6:5-9, I Peter 2:18-29)

VI. We must view ourselves according to our Spiritual Giftedness (1Peter 4:10).
   A. We must see ourselves as servants with gifts to benefit the body (1Peter 4:10-11).
   B. We must know what our gifts are (1Corinthains 12:1-11).
   C. We must use our gifts accordingly (Romans 12:3-8).

Key Point: *Self Esteem is a result not a pursuit. Therefore, Christians should be concentrating on loving God and others in the power of the Holy Spirit and not upon improving their "self-esteem". As he loves consistently, the result will be positive self-esteem. As he is unloving the result will be negative self-esteem. Even though we are not to focus on improving our self-esteem we are called to think soberly about ourselves. This is where we understand the concept of Self-Image. This differs from having dissatisfaction or satisfaction with ourselves (self-esteem). Self-image is the evaluation of how one sees his role and position in life. Also we need to understand that loving self is an implied reality that fits in three categories (Self-centered, Self-Preserving, Soul loving). Once we understand the categories of self-love we will have a better understanding of what it means to deny ourselves (Romans 2:14-17, Proverbs 28:1, Genesis 4:6-7, Romans 12:3, Ephesians 5:28-29) .*

Section Eight

Trials/Suffering/Depression

<u>Trials</u>
(James 1:1-8)

I. Trials expose and develop your <u>*faith*</u> (v1-v3).

   A. Expose <u>*what*</u> you depend on apart from God that you may turn from it and turn to God to build true hope in Him alone.

   B. Expose <u>*who*</u> you depend on apart from God that you may turn from them and turn to God to build true hope in Him alone.

   C. Expose <u>*what*</u> you truly believe about God in real time that you may make the necessary adjustments to build true hope in Him alone.

IV. Trials expose and develop your <u>*endurance*</u> (v3).

   A. Expose how you handle <u>*delays*</u> and teach you how to persevere and stay godly as you work through them.

   B. Expose how you handle <u>*denial*</u> and teach you how to persevere and stay godly as you work through it.

   C. Expose how you handle <u>*disruptions*</u> and teach you how to persevere and stay godly as you work through them.

   D. Expose how you handle <u>*devastations*</u> and teach you how to persevere and stay godly as you work through them.

III. Trials that are endured expose and develop your <u>*character*</u> (v4).

   A. Expose your immature and <u>*sinful*</u> thoughts, words, actions, and expectations towards God and lead you to replace them by developing godly thoughts, words, actions and expectations towards God.

   B. Expose your immature and <u>*sinful*</u> thoughts, words, actions and expectations towards others and lead you to replace them by developing godly thoughts, words, actions, and expectations towards others.

   C. Expose your immature and <u>*sinful*</u> thoughts, words, actions and expectations towards life and lead you to replace them by developing godly thoughts, words, actions, and expectations towards life.

IV. Consider this about your Trials (v5-v8).

    A. If we humble ourselves before God, acknowledge that we need Him and do not stubbornly insist on our way, God will respond by giving us ***Divine*** help to walk in His will through the trial (concept by Jim Berg in <u>When Trouble Comes)</u>.

    B. If we don't believe that God will help us we can't ***expect*** Him to.

    C. If we don't believe that God will help us we will be ***indecisive*** about our choices, ***hesitant*** in our choices, and ***divided*** in our choices as we go back and forth between trusting God and trusting ourselves.

    D. If we don't believe that God will help us we will live a life that is ***unstable, complicated,*** and ***destructive,*** because we know the Truth of God's Word but live by the lies of Satan's world.

Understanding and Dealing With Suffering in Your Life

Definition of suffering: to experience pain or distress as the result of choices within our control and choices beyond our control.

I. **The Reasons We Suffer (Situational Evil, Sin of Self, Sin of Others, Satan, Salvation or Sanctification)**

A. Sometimes we suffer as a result of the ***personal*** sinful choices we make (Galatians 6:7-8, Psalm 38:1-18).

B. Sometimes we suffer as a result of ***people's*** sinful choices against us (Psalm 119:161, 1 Samuel 26:17-25).

C. Sometimes we suffer as a result of ***pursuin***g to be godly in Jesus Christ (2 Timothy 3:12, 1Peter 4:1-3).

D. Sometimes we suffer as a result of ***productivity*** in serving for the sake of Jesus Christ (2 Timothy 4:14-15, Matthew 5:11-12).

E. Sometimes we suffer as a result of God ***pruning*** us so that we may be more productive in serving Him (John 15:2).

F. Sometimes we suffer as a result of the ***perpetrator*** the devil seeking to trouble our lives (Luke 22:31).

G. Sometimes we suffer so that the favor God has shown us doesn't lead us to be ***prideful*** (2Corinthians 12:7).

H. Sometimes we suffer so that we may see the ***proof*** of our faith which should result in character development, perseverance, rejoicing and hope in our Lord and Savior Jesus Christ (1Peter 1: 6-9, James 1:1-5, Romans 5:1-5).

I. Sometimes we suffer as a result of the ***predicaments*** of life beyond our control such as natural disasters or the malfunction of man-made items (Job 1:19, Luke 13:4-5).

J. Some of us suffered the ***piercing*** of others as result of embracing the salvation of Jesus Christ (1 Thessalonians 1:5-7).

II. The Right Perspective to Consider when Suffering

A. We must embrace the fact that God is in **_control_** of all suffering (Ecclesiastes 7:13-14, 9:1).

B. We must embrace the fact that we will not **_escape_** from the experience of suffering in this lifetime (John 16:33).

C. We must embrace the fact that God has already undergone the **_worst_** of all suffering on our behalf (2Corinthains 5:21, 1Peter 2:21-25).

D. We must embrace the fact that God the Son and the God the Holy Spirit are praying on behalf of individuals who **_belong_** to Jesus Christ to God the Father (Romans 8:26-27).

E. We must embrace the fact that God will bring **_good_** (transformation of character into the image of Jesus Christ) out of suffering for the individuals who belong to Jesus Christ (Romans 8:28-32).

F. We must embrace the fact that God will bring **_comfort_** to the people who are His and are suffering as a result of seeking to serve for God's will and good pleasure (2 Corinthians 1:1-7).

G. We must embrace the fact that God will bring the people who are His **_through_** the suffering they encounter accordingly (1 Peter 5:10-11).

H. We must embrace the fact that God will inflict more **_suffering_** on the people who belong to Him when they refuse to turn away from practicing the sin that is currently bringing suffering to their lives (1 Corinthians 11: 27-32).

III. The Right Response to Practice when Suffering

A. We must consider why we are **_suffering_**; Is it due to choices within our control or choices beyond our control? (Situational Evil, Sin of Self, Sin of Others, Satan, Salvation or Sanctification)

B. If our suffering is from the choices we have made to **_disobey_** God in thoughts, desires, motives, or actions we must not be mad at God for the suffering He has allowed, but evaluate at what point we chose to operate apart from seeking to learn or accept the knowledge of God. (Proverbs 19:2-3, 13:15)

C. If our suffering is from the choices we have made to **_disobey_** God in thoughts, desires, motives, or actions then through God's grace we must renounce our sin, repent of our sin, renew our minds in truth, and replace our sin with right living to restore the joy and peace to our lives. (Proverbs 28:13-14, Psalm 51:1-19, 32:1-11)

D. If our suffering is from the choices we have made to **_obey_** God or from choices that are beyond our **_control_**, then through God's grace we must accept what God is allowing while submitting to what God has commanded according to our role and responsibilities, as we endure the suffering. (2 Corinthians 12:7-10)

E. If our suffering is from the choices we have made to **_obey_** God or from choices that are beyond our **_control_**, then through God's grace we must accept the fact that the fullness of God's power reigns in our lives when we suffer for His sake, resulting in Grace (support and kindness), sufficiency (contentment and satisfaction) and humility in our lives. (2Corinthians 12:7-10)

F. If our suffering is from the choices we have made to **_obey_** God or from choices that are beyond our **_control_**, then through God's grace we must accept the fact that God may not remove our affliction that comes from suffering for his sake, but may allow it to stay so that we may experience fullness of God's power resulting in Grace (support and kindness), sufficiency (contentment and satisfaction) and humility in our lives (2Corinthians 12:7-10).

G. We are to **_trust_** God to handle the matters that have consumed us because God thinks about us, concerns Himself with us, and takes interest in us. (1 Peter 5:6-7)

H. We are to be **_clear-headed_**, self- restrained, and keep our minds from anything that will cause confusion as we anticipate the attack of the devil. (1Peter 5:8)

Dealing with Depression

I. The Characterization of Depression

A. An enslaving thought, mood, or feeling of unhappiness which becomes the reason people give for not handling responsibilities, or important issues of life properly or for not handling them at all.

II. The Cause of Depression

A. Depression is the result of unbiblical thinking (1Kings 19:1-18).

B. Depression is the result of responding in sinful thoughts, words or actions to unpleasant or difficult circumstances (Genesis. 4:1-14).

C. Depression is the result of responding to an awareness of personal sin and failure in an ungodly manner (Psalm 32:3-4).

III. The Cure for Depression

A. Identify where you may have been thinking, speaking, or acting in sin towards God in particular situations (Ezra 10:1-2).

B. Identify where you may have been thinking, speaking, or acting in sin towards others in particular situations (Genesis 50:15-21).

C. Identify where you may have been thinking, speaking, or acting in sin in response to unfavorable or difficult circumstances (Psalm 73:1-22).

D. Identify what you want or desire that you cannot control getting from God, others, or circumstances (James 3:13-4:3).

E. Confess and repent of lusting after those wants or desires you cannot control getting from God, others, or circumstances (Proverbs 28:13-14).

F. Confess and repent of ungodly thoughts, words, or actions towards God, others, and circumstances (Psalm 32:1-11, James 5:16).

G. Identify the thoughts, words, actions, or desires God is seeking to develop through your circumstances (James 1:1-8, 1Peter 1:1-9).

H. Discipline yourself to think, behave, and relate in ways that are pleasing to God (Philippians 3:7-21, Ephesians 4:17-32).

I. Identify various ways you can show thanks to God for what He is allowing in your life (1Thessalonians 5:18, Proverbs 17:22).

J. Lay out a daily schedule of task that you are responsible for doing and work on accomplishing them apart from your feelings (Proverbs 16:1,3,9 24:27).

K. Identify some key ways you can serve others and do it apart from your feelings Romans 12:3-21,1Peter 4:10-11).

L. Focus on speaking words that are edifying (Ephesians 4:29).

M. Learn to receive and cultivate hope that comes from trusting God (Romans 5:1-5, Hebrews 6:9-20,1Peter 1:13-16, Hebrews 12:1-3, 1John 3:1-3)

5 <u>Questions to Consider in Evaluating our Situation</u>

1. What is it that God wants me to come to embrace about Him in this situation?

_____
_____
_____

2. What is the biblical view of this situation?

_____
_____
_____

3. What does God want me to see about myself in this situation?

_____
_____
_____

4. What does God want me to learn about others in this situation?

_____
_____
_____

5. What does God want me to do in this situation?

_____
_____
_____

Section Nine

How to Deal With the Past

Presuppositions to Dealing with the Past

A. What has happened to you in the past is not the cause of your bondage to the past. You could not control what happened to you. (Ecclesiastes 7:13-14; 9:1, Job 1:1-2:10)

B. Your present attitudes, words, actions, and desires towards the past are the source of your problems with the past. (Numbers 11:1-6)

C. What you desire from the past situation shapes your perspective and your responses in the present to the past. (Numbers 11:1-6)

D. Since memory is fallible we tend to distort key elements of past situations. (Numbers 11:1-6, Exodus 5:1-23)

E. Learning your patterns of thought, words, actions, desires, and expectations before, during, and after the past experience will help you to deal with the past properly. (Psalm 73)

F. God will allow or cause temporary pain in order to conform us to the image of Christ. (1Peter 1:6-9,5:10, James 1:1-4, Hebrews 12:5-11, Romans 5:1-5, 2Corinthians 4:1-18)

G. The goal of life is not to release you from the pain of your past but for you to develop spiritual maturity through the pain of your past. (Genesis 50:15-20)

H. We are a product of our choices not our past experiences. Therefore experiences are influential not determinative. Your choices have lead you to your bondage not your past. (Galatians 6:7-8)

I. The past is from God and it exist for His glory. (Isaiah 46:9-10)

Process to Dealing with Past

I. **We must identify what we received that we did not want in the past that we still think about with revenge, bitterness, resentment, anger, fear, or worry in the present. (Ruth 1:1-21, 2 Samuel 13:1-29)**
(Naomi-Pleasant/ wanted to change her name to Mara-bitterness- Naomi was bitter because of losing her husband and two children in past experience in Moab while she we was presently in the city of Bethlehem. She received what she did not want from the past and held a bitter attitude in the present.) (Amnon raped Tamar his half-sister, Tamar's brother Absalon held the hatred against Ammon for two years, waited and killed Amnon.)

    A. Did we receive ***rejection or rebuke*** in the past that we still think about with revenge, bitterness, resentment, anger, fear, or worry in the present?

    B. Did we receive ***physical pain or disrespect*** in the past that we still think about with revenge bitterness, resentment, anger, fear, or worry in the present?

    C. Did we receive ***financial lost*** in the past that we still think about with revenge, bitterness, resentment, anger, fear, or worry in the present?

    D. Did we experience the ***death of a loved one*** in the past that we still think about with revenge, bitterness, resentment, anger, fear, or worry in the present?

    E. Did we experience ***abandonment from*** a loved one in the past that we still think about with revenge, bitterness, resentment, anger, fear, or worry in the present?

II. **We must identify what we lost or did not receive in the past that we are still treasuring in our hearts in selfish, self-centered ways in the present (Esther 3:1-11, James 3:13-16, James 4:1-3).**
(Haman's preoccupation with receiving homage from Mordecai which he had not received from the past, lead him to a pursuit of revenge against Mordecai from that point on)

    A. Are we preoccupied with ***acceptance or affirmation*** we lost or did not receive in the past to the point of trying to use God and people to gain it in the present or seeking revenge on others for the past?

    B. Are we preoccupied with ***comfort*** we lost or did not receive in the past to the point of trying use God and people to gain in the present or seeking revenge on others for the past?

    C. Are we preoccupied with ***security*** we lost or did not receive in the past to the point of trying to use God and people to gain it in the present or seeking revenge on others for the past?

D. Are we preoccupied with ***companionship*** we lost or did not receive in the past to the point of trying to use God and people to gain it in the present or seeking revenge on others for the past?

E. Are we preoccupied with ***stability*** we lost or did not receive in the past to the point of trying to use God and people to gain it in the present or seeking revenge on others for the past?

III. **We must confess and repent of the sinful choices we made in the past that has led to the sinful choices and the condition of our life in the present. (2 Samuel 12:1-15, Galatians 6: 7-8, Proverbs 28:13)**
(David confessed his sins to Nathan and before God, yet though he was forgiven, he would suffer negative consequences for a long time.)

A. We must confess and turn away from sinful ***belief systems*** about God, people, and circumstances that has governed our lives in the past and now in the present.

B. We must confess and turn away from the sinful ways of ***communicating*** to and about God, people, and circumstances that has governed our lives in the past and now in the present.

C. We must confess and turn away from the sinful ways of ***living*** before God and in our circumstances that has governed our lives in the past and now in the present.

D. We must confess and turn away from the sinful ways of ***relating*** to God and to others that has governed our lives in the past and now in the present.

IV. **We must interpret our past and live in the present according to the Will of God. (Genesis 50: 15-20, 1Peter 4: 1-11, 1Peter 1:13-16)**
(When Joseph had an opportunity to kill or put his brothers in jail, as a result of putting him in the pit, he forgave them and told them what they meant for evil God had meant for good. He interpreted his situation according to God's will instead his past pain and lived according to God's will.)

A. We must not ask ***why*** did God let those things happen to us; but we must ask how is God using those things that happen to us to bring about the greatest benefit to us and to others and the greatest glory to Himself?

B. We must identify those times in the past where God gave us what we did not ***deserve*** in blessing while choosing not to give us what we did deserve in punishment.

C. We must make present day ***choices*** according to the will of God instead of making present day choices according to the pain of the past.

D. We must ***develop*** in our new life in Christ in the present instead of pursuing the old pleasures from the past.

Dealing with the Past

Introduction: *In dealing with the past we must move beyond the pain and hurt of the experience to address what we desire and who or what we worship because this is what is shaping our response to the past. Therefore, we must take time to identify patterns of thoughts, words, actions, desires, and expectations towards God, people, and circumstances that could be hindering us from moving on from the past. Use these questions as an avenue to examine yourself and ask God for wisdom into the answer to these questions. Journal your answers in a notebook or diary.*

1. What has happen to you?
2. What was your reaction in thought, words, and deeds to God, people in these situations?
3. What did you expect that you did not get from God, people, circumstances?
4. What did you get that did not expect from God, people, and circumstances?
5. What was your view of God before the situation occurred?
6. What was your view of God while the situation was occurring?
7. What was your view of God after the situation occurred?
8. What do you want from God, people, and circumstances in the present so that you can get through the past situation?
9. What feelings about God, people, and circumstances arise when you think about the past situation?
10. Have you considered what God was doing when He allowed this situation to happen to you?
11. How was or is He using the situation from the past to make you more like Christ in the present?
12. What have you learned about your patterns of sin from your past situation?
13. What have you learned about the patterns of God's Grace from your past situation?
14. What have you learned about God's character from your past situation?
15. What have you learned about your character from your past situation?
16. What do you need to change in thoughts, words, actions, expectations in order to grow from the past situation
17. What do you need to change in thoughts, words, actions, expectations in order to draw near to God?
18. Who controls my thoughts, words, actions, expectations?
19. Who is responsible for changing my thoughts, words, actions, expectations?
20. Is there ever a right time to sin against God in thoughts, words, actions?
21. Has God given me the power to obey Him in all circumstances?
22. Has God given me everything I need for life and Godliness?
23. Can I truly do all things through Christ?

Section Ten

Decision Making

Key Point: *We must learn to make good, Godly decisions. In order to do this we must categorize between moral and non-moral issues. Moral issues are spelled out in the bible. These issues are stated as either right or wrong in the Word of God. With these issues you only have to decide if you will or will not obey. Non-moral issues are issues that the bible does not classify as either right or wrong. You have freedom to decide the path you will take. However, the choice must be made in faith or the person is sinning (Romans 14:22-23.) When making decisions on non-moral issues, one has to use wisdom and not allow his freedom to choose become a license to sin (Romans 14; James 4:17).*

1. Some decisions are clearly stated as right and wrong in Scripture. One should decide to obey God's Word by faith (John 14:15).

2. Some decisions are made by one's biblically ordained authority. The biblically ordained authorities are husbands, parents, employers, church leaders, and government. You must comply with their decisions within the parameters of their God-given authority. Therefore, God's will in those situations is that you follow the orders of the authority within the parameters given by God (Ephesians 5:22-6:9, Colossians 3:18-4:1, Titus 2:5-3:2, Hebrews 13:17, 1 Peter 2:13-3:7, Romans 13:1-7).

   a. One should submit even if the decisions seem unreasonable or a matter of preference
   b. (Ephesians 5:24, 1Peter 2:18-20).
   c. One should submit to the decisions while communicating openly in love (Proverbs 27:6a).
   d. One should submit to decisions without attempting to manipulate authority.

<table>
<tr><td colspan="2"><u>Open and Unloving Ways</u></td><td colspan="2"><u>Closed And Unloving Ways</u></td></tr>
<tr><td>1.</td><td>Verbal Anger</td><td>1.</td><td>Physical Withdrawal</td></tr>
<tr><td>2.</td><td>Temper Tantrum</td><td>2.</td><td>Silence</td></tr>
<tr><td>3.</td><td>Physical Violence</td><td>3.</td><td>Flattery</td></tr>
<tr><td>4.</td><td>Making a Public Scene</td><td>4.</td><td>Pouting</td></tr>
<tr><td>5.</td><td>Nagging</td><td>5.</td><td>Uncooperative</td></tr>
<tr><td>6.</td><td>Begging</td><td>6.</td><td>Talking behind back</td></tr>
<tr><td>7.</td><td>Shaming</td><td>7.</td><td>Sighing</td></tr>
<tr><td>8.</td><td>Criticizing</td><td>8.</td><td>Slowing down/stop helping</td></tr>
<tr><td>9.</td><td>Threatening</td><td>9.</td><td>Looking sad</td></tr>
<tr><td>10.</td><td>Bribing</td><td>10.</td><td>Insincere favors or gifts</td></tr>
<tr><td>11.</td><td>Whining</td><td></td><td></td></tr>
<tr><td>12.</td><td>Crying</td><td></td><td></td></tr>
<tr><td>13.</td><td>Going on Strike</td><td></td><td></td></tr>
</table>

e. One should not submit to the decisions if they are in direct violation of the Word of God. Even then one should try to give a biblical alternative before respectfully declining to submit. If necessary, accepting to suffer for righteousness' sake (Acts 4:19; 5:29, Daniel 1:8-13, 1 Peter 3:13-17; 4:12-19).

3. Where the Bible does not categorize an issue as right or wrong you have the freedom to choose preferentially. These are issues that we categorize as non-moral. These issues have no moral implications; the choice is based upon your preference (Romans 14:1-23, 1Corinthians 8:1-13, 1Corinthians 6:12).

4. Although you may have freedom to choose preferentially in issues that are categorized as non-moral, do not allow you freedom to become a license to sin against God by allowing that which you have chosen to lead you into sin. Let your freedom of choice be used as a license to serve God by allowing that which you have chosen to lead you into holy living. i.e. entertainment, food, job, ministry service, husband, wife, church worship (1Corinthians 6:12-20, 1Peter 2:16, Romans 14:13-21, 1Corinthians 8:4-13).

5. These decisions should be made by using biblical principles like the following:
One should make sure that he is controlled by the Holy Spirit (Psalm 66:18, 1 John 1:9, Proverbs 28:13, Ephesians 5:18, Galatians 5:16).
   a. One should identify any and all biblical principles that may apply to the issue (Romans 12:2, 2Timothy 3:16-17, Psalm 1:1-3, Proverbs 19:2-3).
   b. One should seek to gather as much relevant data as possible.(i.e. books, magazines, articles, website info etc.) (Proverbs 14:8,15, 16).
   c. One should seek wisdom from persons who are knowledgeable in that area in which they are seeking to make decisions. One should get counsel and information. One should not seek to let the person to make a decision for them (Proverbs 11:14, Proverbs 20:5, Proverbs 19:20, Proverbs 15:22).
   d. Once should weigh the pros and cons of his alternatives and then make a decision according to the alternative that seems to have more pros than cons (Proverbs 14:15-16).
   e. One must accept by faith that he has not sinned in his choice. One must accept the consequences that come with the choice (Proverbs 16:1, 9).
   f. One must accept that God will either allow it to go forward as chosen or God may re-direct as He sees fit (We choose God decides) (Proverbs 16: 1, 9 James 4:13-17).

(Information adapted from Rich Thomson)

Decision Making

1. Identify the issue whereby you have to make a decision.

   _____

   _____

   _____

   _____

   _____

2. Determine if the issue is a moral or non- moral issue.

   _____

   _____

   _____

   _____

3. Determine if the issue is to be addressed by those who are in authority over you.

   _____

   _____

   _____

   _____

4. Research the scripture to see what it has to say on the issue both directly and indirectly. Write down what you find.

   _____

   _____

   _____

   _____

5. Research any and all forms of information to gather relevant data on the issue. Write down what you find.

   _____

   _____

   _____

   _____

6. Talk with people who have expertise on this issue and write down what you find.

   _____

   _____

   _____

   _____

   _____

7. Identify the pros and cons of each alternative and write down what you find.

_____
_____
_____
_____
_____
_____

8. Make a decision in faith. Write down your decision and explain why you chose that alternative instead the other alternatives.

_____
_____
_____
_____
_____
_____
_____

Section Eleven

Living by Purpose

(Proverbs 14:8 – "The wisdom of the prudent is to understand his way; but the folly of fools is deceit.")

I. **The Principle of Living by Purpose**
   A. Scripture calls for human planning while acknowledging God's sovereignty (Proverbs 20:5,18,15:22,26,16:1,3,9,19:21, 21:5, 24:8 and James 4:13-17).
   B. Decisions are to be made understanding:
      1. the moral will of God – the areas of life where Scripture has stated what we are to do and not to do (2Timothy 3:16-17, James 1:19-27, John 14:21, Romans 12:1-21,13:1-14);
      2. the sovereign will of God – the reality that God controls all things and is working out his overall plan for the universe (Ecclesiastes 7:13-14, Lamentations 3:37-38, Colossians1:15-17, Ephesians 1:9-10, 2Peter 3:1-18);
      3. the non moral will of God – the areas of life where Scripture gives no specific instructions or commands and we are free to choose what we desire, being considerate of your loyalty of God and love for others (1Corinthians 6:12,8:4-13, Romans 14:1-23).
   C. Life is to be arranged according to God's priorities Matthew 22:34-40).
   D. Life is to be arranged with relationships in mind (John 13:34-35, Romans 12:3-1).
   E. Life is to be lived according to God's values (Luke 6:20-49, 12:13-34).

II. **The Prerequisites of Living by Purpose**
   A. We must learn the character of God and His plan for mankind.
   B. We must study God's agenda for every aspect of life.
   C. We must become aware of our personalities, spiritual gifts, natural talents and treasures and learn how to use them to God's Glory.
   D. We must identify the people, places, things, and activities we are to manage.
   E. We must learn where we are to lead and where we are to follow.

III. **The Process of Living by Purpose**
   A. Identify the various roles you have in life.
   B. Identify which roles are God given, man given and self given and determine the roles you must keep and the ones you must let go.
   C. Identify the Biblical Mandates and the responsibilities that are associated with each role.
   D. Organize your roles according to God's priorities.
   E. Identify what you are to accomplish in each particular role and the steps its going to take to accomplish these things.

F. Write out the specific task you have to do on a daily or weekly basis to accomplish what needs to be accomplished.
G. Write out specific ways you can use your spiritual gifts and natural talents to serve your family, the Body of Christ and others accordingly on a daily or weekly basis.

Take some time and work through the questions.

1. Who is God and what is His Mission?

_____

_____

2. What are your spiritual gifts, natural talents and personality type?

_____

_____

3. What are the various roles and responsibilities you have right now in life?

_____

_____

4. Looking at your spiritual gifts, natural talents, treasures, temple, personality, roles and responsibilities how do you believe God wants you to join Him in His Mission?

_____

_____

_____

5. How will you prioritize and organize your roles, responsibilities, spiritual gifts, and natural talents to accomplish what God wants you to accomplish?

_____

_____

6. Who has God placed in authority over you to hold you accountable?

_____

_____

7. Who has God placed under your authority to hold accountable?

_____

_____

8. Looking at our spiritual gifts, natural talents, treasures, personalities, and natural talents within our family what is God's Mission for this family?

_____

_____

9. Looking at our spiritual gifts, treasures, personalities, and natural talents within our family what are the specific things we need to do to accomplish what God wants us to do for each other in the family and for others?

_____

_____

10. How will this family do what we need to do in order to accomplish what God wants us to do for each other and for others?

_____

_____

11. What will be the responsibilities of all in the family to accomplish what God wants us to do for each other and for others?

_____

_____

12. Who will hold us accountable to do what we need to do in our family?

_____

_____

13. What ministries and organizations do we need to involve ourselves in?

_____

_____

14. What ministries and organizations do we need to let go of?

_____

_____

After working through the information above write a job description for each role you play with Scripture to validate the role.

Job Description

Position Title:_____

Purpose of the Position:_____ Scripture:

Reports to:_____

Relates Closely to:_____

Responsible for:

- _____ *Scripture:*
- _____ *Scripture:*
- _____ *Scripture:*
- _____ *Scripture:*
- _____ *Scripture:*
- _____ *Scripture:*
- _____ *Scripture:*

Measurable Goals for the Position

- _____
- _____
- _____
- _____
- _____
- _____
- _____

Here is an example to consider:

POSITION TITLE: Husband/Father

PURPOSE OF THE POSITION: To lead, love, feed, watch over, protect and serve immediate family and those of the Household (1Cor 11:3, Eph 5:25-27, 1Tim 5:8, John 13:1-17, 1John 3:16, Acts 20:28).

REPORTS TO: Jesus Christ, Elders, Accountability Couple

RELATES CLOSELY WITH: Wife, Daughter, Accountability Couple, Mother, Father, Mother in Law and Father in Law

RESPONSIBLE FOR:
- Leading family in the direction designed by God for this family (Joshua 24:14-15).
- Setting an example for Godly living (Matthew 5:6, 1Timothy 4:16).
- Establishing a system for discipling the family to spiritual maturity (Ephesians 5:25-27,6:4, Hebrews 10:24, Proverbs 22:6, 1Corinthians 14:35).
- Providing financial provisions to meet the basic needs of the immediate family and household (1Timothy 5:8, 1John 3:16-19).
- Establishing guidelines and goals for every aspect of living in the home that are according to God's Standards and God's Design for the Family (1Timothy 3:4-5).
- Providing support and service to all members in the household in order that they may live out the purpose God designed for each individual in the household (Romans 12:9-13, Hebrews 3:12-13).
- Protecting the family against hurt, harm, and danger (1John 3:16, Acts 20:28).
- Providing sexual fulfillment to wife unconditionally (1Corinthians 7:1-5).

CONTINUING RESPONSIBILITIES:
- Assisting in handling household responsibilities (Philippians 2:3-4).
- Tracking the spiritual growth of the immediate family and household (John 21:15-17).
- Honoring, Praising, and Showing appreciation to my wife on a consistent basis (Proverbs 31:28, 1Peter 3:7).
- Establishing and providing opportunities for family fun, fellowship and travel (Acts 2:42, Hebrews 10:25).
- Seeking to constantly understand who my wife is and how to serve and honor her accordingly (1Peter 3:7).

Measurable Goals for the Position
- What life skills are being developed in my life and family?
- What needs am I meeting for my wife, children and others right now?
- What commitments am I keeping?
- What household responsibilities am I maintaining?
- What social events/hobbies have we been involved in?
- What trips have we taken?

- What level of spiritual maturity is found in my family?
- Whose burdens are we bearing and needs are we meeting for one another and those outside the family?
- What have I protected my family from?
- What financial provisions are being made for my family?
- How much debt are we going into?
- How much debt are we coming out of?
- What goals have we set and accomplished as a family /as individuals in the family?
- What souls have been saved as a result of our family?
- What lives have grown spiritually as result of our family?

POSITION TITLE: Wife

PURPOSE OF THE POSITION: To support and help her husband in various ways so that he may be and do all God designed for him (Genesis 2:18-22).

REPORTS TO: God, Husband, Church Leaders

RELATES CLOSELY WITH: Husband, Daughter, Mother, Father, Mother in law and father in law

RESPONSIBLE FOR:
- Submitting to husband in every aspect of life as unto the Lord (Eph 5:23, Titus 2:3-5,1Peter 3:1)
- Helping her husband in those areas of his life where he is unable to function adequately (Genesis 2:18)
- Meeting his needs in every aspect of the Marriage (Philippians 2:3-4, 1Peter 4:10)
- Showing respect to her husband (Ephesians 5:33)
- Keeping the home inviting and orderly (Titus 2:3-5 Psalm 128:3 Proverbs 31:27)
- Assisting her husband in the raising of children (Titus 2:3-5, Psalm 128:3)
- Keeping herself beautiful inside and outside (1Peter 3:3-5)
- Providing sexual fulfillment to her husband unconditionally (1Corinthians 7:1-5)
- Using her skills, talents, gifts to support her husband and family as first priority   (Proverbs 31:27, Psalm128:3, Titus 2:3-5)
- Being loyal, trustworthy, and dependable in attitude, action, and service to her husband in every aspect of the relationship (Proverbs 31:10-12)

Measurable Goals
- In what ways am I submitting to my husband?
- How am I using my strengths to compensate for my husband's weaknesses?
- What needs am I meeting of my husband?
- What ways am I showing respect to my husband?
- Am I keeping the home inviting and orderly?
- What ways am I helping my husband raise our children?
- What am I doing to keep myself attractive for my husband?

- Is my husband satisfied sexually by me?
- What gifts, talents, skills, and resources am I using to support my Husband/my family?

Position Title: Child

Purpose of the Position: to obey and honor our parents according to God's standard (Ephesians 6:1-13)

Reports to: Parents & God

Responsible For:
- Respecting them (Ephesians 6: 1-13, Colossians 3:20, 1 Peter 1:14)
- Maintaining responsibilities as assigned & doing what needs to be done with a right attitude (Ephesians 6: 1-13, Colossians 3:20)
- Supporting and Encouraging them accordingly (Ephesians 6:1-13, Colossians 3:20)
- Getting a clear understanding of what the instruction is that have been given which includes knowing what they expect and following those instructions accordingly
- Maintaining my household chores accordingly (knowing how to clean according to my parents standards)

Measurable Goals For The position:
- How am I showing respect to my parents?
- How am I being supportive to our parents?
- What ways am I encouraging my parents on a daily basis?
- What has been my attitude when doing what has been asked of me?
- What am I doing to develop a proper relationship with my parents?
- What did I do without being asked to do so?
- What instructions have I been following?
- What household responsibilities am I faithfully taking care of?

After working through the information above write a mission plan for your life.

Purpose of Existence (Why Do I exist?)
_____
_____

Objectives (What specific ways am I to join God in His Mission?)
_____
_____
_____
_____
_____

Process (What steps do I take to accomplish what I need to accomplish?)
_____
_____
_____
_____

Resources (Who and What Do I have and need to accomplish my objectives ?)
_____
_____
_____
_____

Here is an example to consider.

Mission Plan

Purpose of Existence (*Why Do I exist?*)
To lead, love, feed, watch over, protect and serve immediate family, those of my household, those under my care at the College of Biblical Studies and those under my care at Jireh Bible Church.

Objectives (*What specific ways am I to join God in His Mission?*)
1. To lead family in the direction designed by God for this family (Joshua 24:14-15).
2. To set an example for Godly living (Matthew 5:6, 1Timothy 4:16).
3. To establish a system for discipling the family to spiritual maturity (Eph 5:25-27, 6:4, Hebrews 10:24, Proverbs 22:6, 1Corinthians 14:35).
4. To provide financial provisions to meet the basic needs of the immediate family and household (1Timothy 5:8, 1John 3:16-19).
5. To establish guidelines and goals for every aspect of living in the home that are according to God's Standards and God's Design for the Family (1Timothy 3:4-5).
6. To provide support and service to all members in the household in order that they may live out the purpose God designed for each individual in the household (Romans 12:9-13, Hebrews 3:12-13).
7. To protect the family against hurt, harm, and danger (1John 3:16, Acts 20:28).
8. To proclaim the Gospel of Jesus Christ (2Timothy 4:1-5).
9. To teach Men, Women, Children how to obey God (Matthew 28:18-20).
10. To equip Men, Women, and Children to serve according to their giftedness and to relate to one another in love (Ephesians 4:11-16, 1Timohty 1:5).
11. To make sure the needs of the church and students are taking care of (Titus 3:14).
12. To make sure the Church and the class room is pure and sin is addressed (1Corinthians 5, Galatians 6:1-2).
13. To make sure the doctrines, disciplines, and duties of the Christian faith are properly proclaimed to the Church and the students (2Timothy 4:1-5).
14. To develop and select spiritual leaders to assist in taking care of the Church and the students (1Timohty 3:1-13).

Process (*What steps do I take to accomplish what I need to accomplish?*)
1. Organize my time by my roles and responsibilities.
2. Have two days for just my wife and daughter that I maintain.
3. Find faithful, available, and teachable men to groom to assist in the process caring for the church and my students.
4. Develop a once a month get away to relax and renew.
5. Find curriculum and books that I can read that will help me to grow in my faith.

6. Find an older man to hold me accountable and teach me according to their wisdom and knowledge.

Resources (*Who and What Do I have and need to accomplish my objectives*)
1. I have my wife to support me.
2. I have my daughter to support me.
3. I have been trained by Dallas Seminary and the Master's College and several Pastors in the community.
4. I have the support of my parishioners and students.
5. I need more education in biblical counseling to enhance my serving of others.
6. I need an older man to tutor me spiritual development and pasturing.
7. I need someone to teach me how to invest so that I may retire debt free and have money to live on.
8. I need some faithful, available, teachable men that I can train to lead and take over
9. Various parts of the ministry and soon to take my place.

After working through the information above write a mission plan for your family.

Purpose of Existence (Why Did God allow my family to Exist?)

_____

_____

Objectives (What are specific ways our family is join God in His Mission?)

_____

_____

_____

_____

Responsibilities (What is each person in the family responsible for doing to accomplish our assignment?)

_____

_____

_____

_____

Process (What steps do we need to take to accomplish our assignment as a family?)

_____

_____

_____

_____

Accountability (Who will hold us accountable?)

_____

_____

_____

_____

Measurable Goals (How will we measure our progress?)

_____

_____

_____

Here is an example to consider.

The Ellen Family
(*Mission Plan*)

Purpose Statement: **To be a family unit that uses their God-given abilities to help each other function as God designed and disciple families abroad.**

Objectives of Family:
1. To bear on another's burdens.
2. To meet one another's needs.
3. To help each other grows in obedience to God.
4. To help each other grows in love for all.
5. To disciple married couples.
6. To disciple men and women according to God's leading.
7. To serve various churches and Christian organizations through our various gifts, talents, and treasures.
8. To help hurting people on a city-wide level and abroad.

Process:
1. Nicolas and Venessa will lay out monthly responsibilities according to the various roles each person in the family holds.
2. Through monthly family meetings we will discover what needs, concerns, and interest we need to address with each other and make sure that they are taken care of within a timely manner.
3. Nicolas will select the discipleship material according to individual needs of each person in the family and train them through it accordingly.
4. Venessa will develop and maintain a family budget and manage the finances.
5. Venezia will take care of household responsibilities as assigned by Venessa.
6. Nicolas and Venessa will use their biblical counseling training to disciple men/women and married couples.
7. Nicolas and Venessa will develop a home for unwed pregnant women and a biblical counseling center to help people city-wide and abroad.
8. Nicolas and Venessa will work with local seminaries, Christian organizations, and Christian Schools to teach and serve according to their resources.
9. Venezia will use her gifts, talents, and treasures to bear burdens, meet needs, and teach truth to her friends, relatives, school mates, and people abroad.
10. Venezia will seek to work with children via volunteering at local organizations, baby sitting, and through her vocation.
11. The family will seek to have monthly times of fun and fellowship with each other and friends.
12. The family will take annual vacations for fun and fellowship.

Accountability Partners:
1. Ira and Cynthia will hold us accountable in our marriage relationship.
2. Pastor Rich will hold us accountable to living responsibly as individuals in Christ.
3. Our Pastor will hold us accountable as a family to live responsibly in Christ.

Measurable Goals:
1. What life skills and spiritual truths are being developed in my family?
2. What needs and burdens are we addressing of each other?
3. What household responsibilities am I maintaining?
4. What social events/hobbies have we been involved in?
5. What trips have we taken?
6. What is our financial status?
7. What goals have we set and accomplished as a family /as individuals in the family?
8. What souls have been saved as a result of our family?
9. What lives have grown spiritually as result of our family?

After working through the information above develop a weekly/ daily task sheet according to your roles and responsibilities.

Roles	Task for Sunday	Task for Monday	Task for Tuesday	Task For Wednesday	Task for Thursday	Task for Friday	Task for Saturday

Here is an example:

Roles	Task for Sunday	Task for Monday	Task for Tuesday	Task For Wednesday	Task for Thursday	Task for Friday	Task for Saturday
Husband	Have a talk time to discuss some problems Go to a movie/dinner and hang out		Make sure I take the cars to be washed			Take wife out to dinner and a movie and hang out	Help her with some of the work around House
Father			Take my daughter to school and talk with her about he life Talk with Daughter about some Guy she seems to like	Take my daughter to school and talk with her about he life Discuss her progress through the book of Ephesians	Take my daughter to school and talk with her about he life Discuss the worksheet called Why does man need God		Take daughter and friend to movie and hang out
Pastor	Finish out sermon series/ try to finish Sunday school lesson	Prepare Sunday's and Wednesday's Lesson Pre pare for counseling sessions for today Follow up with a phone call on visitors	Prepare Sunday's and Wednesday's Lesson Pre pare for counseling sessions for today	Prepare Sunday's and Wednesday's Lesson Pre pare for counseling sessions for today	Prepare Sunday's Lesson and Sunday School's lesson Pre pare for counseling sessions for today		Prepare Sunday's Lesson and Sunday School's lesson
Teacher		Prepare and Teach Ms 4344	Prepare and Teach Ms 4345		Prepare and teach Ms 405 Counseling		Prepare and Teach Ms 405 Counseling
Son	Call parents and say hello						
Student		Read Ch 1 and do worksheet					

93

Books to Study:

The Knowledge of The Holy by A.W. Tozer
Desiring God by John Piper
Faith in Future Grace by John Piper
What a Way to Live(The Kingdom Agenda) by Tony Evans
Discovering your God Given Gifts Don and Katie Fortune
Decision Making in the Will of God by Gary Freison
How Now Shall We Live (workbook) by Charles Colson
Experiencing Christ Within by Dwight Edwards
The Mind of Christ (workbook) by TW Hunt
How Can I Change? By C. J. Mahoney
The Exemplary Husband by Stuart Scott
The Excellent Wife by Martha Peace
Your Family God's Way by Wayne Mack
Christian Living in Your Home by Jay Adams
The Age of Opportunity by Paul David Tripp
Strengthening Your Marriage by Wayne Mack
Shepherding a Child's Heart by Paul David Tripp
War of Words by Paul David Tripp
Created for His Glory by Jim Berg
Changed Into His Image by Jim Berg

Section Twelve

The Cycle of Relationships

The Cycle of Self-Centered Relationships

Pride is a mind set on self with resistance to the will and ways of God. This leads to evaluating and dealing with people according to your own estimations, leading to various relational problems (Prov. 3:5-8, 28:26, 14:12).

As you function in pride, you tend to develop a picture of people in accordance to your opinion, resulting in an inevitable cycle:

Picture →	Preference →	Presumption →	Pain →	Practice
You have a settled opinion about a person's: -Character -Conduct -Conversation -Commitments -Care -Compassion -Concern in relation to self, God, others, and life situations. The problem with your settled opinion is that sometimes it's true/ sometimes it's false.	You are consumed with: ways you want the person to function in: -Character -Conduct -Conversations -Commitments - ways you want the person to commit to and care about you and others. -ways you want this person to be concerned about you and others; to be compassionate towards you and others.	You make judgments or assumptions about the person's: - Motives - Desires -Words - Actions in a situation or matter that has not proven to be true at the moment; it is an assessment and interpretation based on your picture and preference of that person at that moment.	You experience -Disappointment -Anger -Grief -Sadness -Discontentment You experience these emotions as a result of what you are thinking. Your thinking is dominated by your picture, preference, and presumption of the person resulting in the pain your are experiencing.	You treat the person poorly as a result of your: -Picture of them, -Preference of them, -Presumption of them, -Pain with them You ignore God's precept on how to treat the person because you are not operating out of humility and love; you are operating out of pride and lust as a result, you feel justified in your actions.
He who trust in his own heart is a fool, but he who walks wisely will be delivered (Prov. 28:26).	Therefore do not let what is for you a good thing be spoken of as evil (Rom 14:16).	There is a way which seems right to a man but its end is the way of death (Prov. 14:12).	The heart knows its own bitterness, and a stranger does not share its joy (Prov. 14:10).	Every prudent man acts with knowledge, But a fool displays folly (Prov. 13:16).

The Cycle of Christ-Centered Relationships

Humility is a mind set on Christ with a submission to the will of God. This leads to evaluating life, God, and people according to the Word of God (Romans 12:2, Philippians 2:3-5).

As you function in humility you tend to see people according to their position before God and their position before you resulting in an inevitable cycle.

Position →	Priority →	Precept →	Peace →	Practice
You evaluate a person according to his/ her position. Before God they are either: -saved -Unsaved Before you they are either: -in authority over you, -a subordinate to you, -a colleague equal to you	You focus on how God wants a person to present and demonstrate their : -Character -Conduct -Conversation -Commitment -Care -Compassion -Concern- You focus on how a person may please God instead of focusing on how they may please you.	You evaluate a matter with a person according to truth in four categories : -Is this a preference issue? -Is this a wisdom issue? -Is this a conscience issue? - Is this a sin issue? You evaluate a matter with a person in truth according to their position before God and their position before you. -is this an opportunity to share the Gospel? -is this an opportunity to lead, follow, or serve?	You experience Tranquility of soul in spite of difficulty with a person as a result evaluating the matter according to truth.	You relate with a person according to your role and responsibility. If they are under you, you look after and lead in love. If they are over you, you line up with and be loyal to in love. If they are equal to you, you serve and give preference to in love. Your role and responsibility determines how you treat he person. Matters are handled by God's Commands.
Wisdom is in the presence of one who has understanding, but the eyes of a fool are on the ends of the earth (Prov. 17:24).	**We proclaim Him, admonishing every man and teaching every man with all wisdom, so that we may present every man complete in Christ. (Col 1:28).**	**From your precepts I get understanding, Therefore I hate every false way. (Psalm 119:104).**	**Those who love Your law have great peace, and nothing can make them stumble . (Ps. 119:165).**	**Every prudent man acts with knowledge, but a fool displays folly. (Prov. 13:16).**

Section Thirteen

Abuse, Separation, Divorce, Remarriage

Key Point: *We cannot control what people think say or do. We are responsible for how we respond to people and situations. We do not have control over a disobedient spouse. We can only control our response to a disobedient spouse. If we at anytime are doing wrong to make our spouse do right we are sinning. The end does not justify the means. Therefore, in the situation of physical abuse, the abused spouse must do what is right in the sight of God even though the abuser is not. The abused spouse is free to find safety away from the abuser without violating the marital covenant made with the abuser. Physical abuse is not a ground for divorce; this is why the abused has the freedom to find safety away from the abuser without violating the marital covenant with the abuser. Separation is only permissible for a short time, to deal with safety matters for the one who is being abused and to regroup in order to face the issues within the marriage, not a way to get out of the marriage. When people are separated they are still married. Separation is not divorce therefore; you are still obligated to each other as a husband and wife. You cannot be separated for a long time and fulfill the commands of God in relation to the marital covenant.*

When a person is being abused there are several ways they can work through the situation such as:

1. Lovingly confronting the abuser about the situation. They must do so making sure they have addressed their own unloving thoughts, words, or actions that may be involved in the situation before confronting the person. The abuser does not have the right to abuse the person regardless to how the one being abused may have contributed or reacted to the abuse. But the person being abused still has to address their response or contribution to the situation before confronting the abuser. If the abuser is unwilling to repent the person being abused must call in others to assist in the matter. If the abuser does not respond to this they must call in Church leadership as well (Matthew 7:1-5, 18:15-17).

2. Calling the police to handle the situation accordingly (Romans 13:1-7).

3. Finding safety away from the abuser without violating the marital covenant with the abuser. Abuse is not a justification for divorce therefore, one cannot use divorce as a way of escape from abuse (Proverbs 22:3, Proverbs 27:12).

4. Entrusting themselves to God by doing what is right in the marriage. This means the abused is responsible for still doing what they are called to do within a marriage while finding safety away from the abuser (Proverbs 15:1, 1Peter 3:1, 1Peter 3:13-17, Proverbs 22:3, 27:12).

5. Separation is only permissible for a short time, to deal with safety matters for the one who is being abused and to regroup in order to face the issues within the marriage; not to get out of the marriage. The husband and wife must continue to do what God called them to do within the marital covenant. When people are separated they are still married. Therefore, they must follow the commands of Scripture by doing what God has designed for a husband and wife. Therefore, you cannot stay away from each other for a long period time and fulfill your responsibilities as a husband and wife. As long as one is married they are called to function according to what is below. Too much time apart means that one cannot fulfill these responsibilities. This calls for repentance and return to their God-given responsibilities with each other knowing that suffering may come in doing so. Yet, the one who has been abused is to do what is right while still pursuing safety accordingly. This is a difficult and delicate balance (Proverbs 22:3, Proverbs 27:12, Proverbs 15:1, 1Peter 2:13-25, 1Thessalonians 5:18, 1 Peter 3:1-7,13-17, Ephesians 5:18-33, 1Corinthians 7:1-5, Titus 2:4-5,).

Husbands are to love their wives (Ephesians 5:25-30).

- Meaning—to self sacrifice for the benefit, provision, welfare of his wife in all aspects of her life (Ephesians 5:25-31).
- Manner—as Christ loved the Church (Ephesians 5:25-31).
- Motive—to help her to become Holy/Blameless; that she may function according to God's design (Ephesians 5:25-31).
- Magnitude—to death (1John 3:16-18).
- Manifestation—considering her interest concerns, needs, desires, and making sure they are taken care of in the way that Christ would do it for the Church; relating with her socially, spiritually, emotionally, and sexually in a manner that benefits her and reflects the character of Christ; compensating for her weaknesses in ways that Christ would do it for the Church; leading and guiding her into spiritual maturity, helping her to be all of what God designed her to be in the way that Christ would do it for the Church; leading your wife as Christ would lead the Church in all aspects of the marriage (1 Peter 3:7, 1 Corinthians 7:33).

Wives are to submit to their husbands (Ephesians 5:22-24).

- Meaning—to willingly follow the leadership of your husband; to willingly follow the instructions of your husband (Ephesians 5:22-24).
- Manner—as the Church submits to Christ the Lord; as if she were responding to Jesus Christ Himself (Ephesians 5:22-24).
- Motive—out of respect for God's design (Ephesians 5:22-24).
- Magnitude—in everything that is not sin including Preferences (Ephesians 5:22-24).

- Manifestation—following her husband's leadership and directives in all that she does in the home and outside the home as unto the Lord; following her husband's leadership and directives in the raising of the children as unto the Lord; showing respect to her husband in all aspects of the marriage as unto the Lord; managing their home in ways that is in line with her husband's leadership and directives as unto the Lord; listening to and following through on the things that concern your husband that has been requested of you as unto the Lord (Titus 2:3-5, Proverbs 31:10-31, 1 Corinthians 7:34, 1 Peter 3:1-6).

Key Point: *As we look at divorce and remarriage we must evaluate a few key items and evaluate what is the best course of action. Reconciliation is the optimal choice. However, people do not always do what is optimal. If a person has divorced and is looking to remarry we must evaluate the nature of the divorce to determine if remarriage would be proper within the context of the situation.*

Considerations for Divorce and Remarriage

1. God's desire for husband and wife is to stay married. Sexual sin was the grounds mentioned in the New Testament for a permissible divorce for God's people. Even then if reconciliation is possible it should be done. (Matthew 19:1-9, Luke 17:1-3).

2. If a believer refuses to stay married to another believer and gets a divorce from that spouse for reasons other than adultery by their spouse, they are to stay single or be reconciled to that spouse in marriage. If they repent, seek to return to the marriage and that spouse has moved on the leadership must decide if remarriage to another Christian is possible (1Corinthians 7:10-11, Hebrews 13:17).

3. If a believer is married to an unbeliever and that unbeliever decides to leave the marriage the believer is free to file for divorce or accept the divorce from the unbeliever. However if a believer has a spouse that is an unbeliever that wants to stay in the marriage accordingly (not stay married yet live in sexual sin with other people) they must remain in the marriage (1Corinthians 7:12-16).

4. A believer is free to divorce their spouse and remarry another Christian if their spouse has committed adultery (Matthew 19:1-9, 2Corinthians 6:14-18).

5. A believer who has been married and divorced before he became a Christian is free to remarry since that happened before he/she was a Christian. He is considered a new creature in Christ with new privileges to stay single or to be married to a believer. They cannot return to their formal unbelieving spouse because they are now Christians (Christians are not to marry unbelievers.) (2Corinthians 5:16-17, 1Corinthains 7:20-40, 2Corinthians 6:14-18).

6. If a believer is in an unbiblical marriage they must repent of the sin while remaining faithful to the person they are married to (Proverbs 28:13-14, 1Corinthaisn 7:10-11).

(Material adapted from Rich Thomson in His Book <u>The Heat of Man and The Mental Disorders</u> Bill Shannon Till Death Do Us Part: A Biblical Look at Divorce & Remarriage Pastor of Children's Ministry at Grace Community Church Sun Valley, California.)

Section Fourteen

Death, Grief, Despair, Biblical View of Illness, Psychotropic Drugs and Biblical Counseling

Death & Grief & Despair

I. Key Points about Grief (*1Thessalonians 4:13-18*)
- A. Grieving is impacted by one's hope or lack thereof.
- B. Hope must be developed; it will not come haphazardly.
- C. As one studies and embraces the Word of God he will develop true hope in the mist of grief.

II. Key Points about Despair (*Proverbs 17:22*)
- A. When one is despairing they are viewing the reality of life without God; they have grief without hope (Concept adapted from Jim Berg.)
- B. When one is despairing they are not accepting or embracing the sufficiency and sovereignty of God.
- C. When one is despairing they are not understanding or considering the nature of death, burial and resurrection of Jesus Christ and its' correlation to life and death for those who belong to Jesus Christ.

III. Key Points about Grief in Relation to Death (*1Thessalonians 4:13-18*)
- A. One who is grieving is feeling and expressing genuine sorrow with biblical hope.
- B. One who is grieving with biblical hope is accepting and embracing the sufficiency and sovereignty of God.
- C. One who is grieving with biblical hope considers and accepts the hope that rest on the death, burial, and resurrection of Jesus Christ.

IV. Things that tend to show up when a person Grieves (*Proverbs 13:12*)
- A. Grief tends to take us out of our normal element of acting and reacting.
- B. A grieving person may start to react in ways they do not seem normal to who they are.
- C. Whatever was really on the inside of the person begins to appear during the time of grieving; If there were any unresolved issue or concerns between the person and the deceased it may show up during the time of grieving:
    1. Hostility
    2. Guilt
    3. Anger
    4. Fear
    5. Bitterness
    6. Resentment

V. Stages of Grief: Adapted by Jay Adams (*Proverbs 13:12*)

Shock:
- Bewilderment
- Numbness
- Feeling of being stunned
- Hysteria
- Near or actual paralysis
- What was held on the inside will manifest in words and actions on the outside
- Physically Present but not verbally interacting with anyone

Disorganization:
- Physical Distress
- Drained emotions state of being
- Feelings of emptiness
- A sense of non-reality
- Going through the motions in their life duties
- Loss of spirit, rest, joy and or initiative or motivation
- Becoming stiff and formal towards close friends or family
- May act standoffish seeming not to care
- May act discourteous
- Realization that life will be different starts to sink in
- The uncertainty of new direction may cause fear where faith is lacking
- A time where things come apart
- A time where things come out in the open that have been held in
- A whole life comes under review
- Begin to take a new look at self, life, death etc.

Reorganization:
- Others have moved on and forgotten
- Decision must be made about their new direction
- Tired, confused, somewhat fearful
- Begins the process of laying the foundation to begin a new life

VI. Insight on How to deal with someone who is Grieving: (Adapted from Jay Adams)
   (*1 Thessalonians 5:14*)

A. When they are in shock say very little (Job 2:11-13).

B. Get the suffering person to talk about their relationship with deceased, their view of God and their view of death when the time is right (Proverbs 20:5).

C. As they are talking, look for signs of guilt, fear, anger, resentment, hostility, unresolved issues with deceased person, bad relationship patterns with the deceased, bitterness or bad relating patterns with others (Luke 6:45).

D. Do not minimize their negative evaluation of self (Luke 6:45).

E. If you identify signs of sin between the suffering person and God or the suffering person and the deceased or the suffering person and others, help them move into the following: (Galatians 6:1-2)

    1. Confession and repentance
    2. Forgiveness
    3. Restitution
    4. Reconciliation

F. Give them a biblical view of grief (1 Thessalonians 4:13-18).

G. Instill hope in their hearts by discussing the following: (1 Thessalonians 4:13-18)

    1. The blessing of eternal life (John 3:16-18).
    2. The resurrection of our bodies (1 Corinthians 15:1-58).
    3. The reunion of believers in heaven (1 Thessalonians 4:13-18).
    4. The anticipation of living in the presence of Christ (2 Corinthians 5:1-6).

H. Help the person get biblical objectives for the future (Philippians 3:1-21).

I. Help the person list problems specifically that they must overcome to reach their new objectives (Proverbs 22:3).

J. Discuss biblical solutions to those difficulties that must be overcome to reach their objectives (Proverbs 19:20-21).

K. Help the person lay out a plan of action and walk with them through the plan (Proverbs 20:5).

Scriptures to Consider

Genesis 3:19 – Returning to the grounds
Ecclesiastes 8:8 – Death a way for all
Hebrews 9:27 – Judgment after death
Deuteronomy 32:39 – Death ordered by God
2Corinthians 5:1 – The earthly tent being dissolved
2Peter 1:14 – Putting off this tabernacle
Genesis 49:33 – Will be gathered to our people
Romans 6:16, 21, 8:13, - The necessary consequences of sin
Romans 6:23 – The wages of sin is death
Matthew 25:46 – Righteous will have eternal life
John 3:16, 8:21 – Eternal life
Revelation 2:11, 20:6 – A Christian way of escape
1Corinthians 15: 1-58 – New Glorified Bodies
1John 3:1-3 – The return of Christ and our benefit

(Information Adapted from Biblical Counseling Manuel by Jay Adams)

A Biblical View and Response to Physical Illness and Christians on Psychotropic Drugs

I. The Biblical View of Physical Illness
   A. Illness exist because of the fall of Adam which resulted in the curse of sin on our lives leading to weak and frail bodies (Romans 5:12, 1Peter 1:24).
   B. Illness may occur due to unconfessed sin in ones' life (Psalm 32:1-4).
   C. Illness may occur because God is punishing an unbeliever (Exodus 15:26).
   D. Illness may occur because God is disciplining a believer (2Samuel 12:14-15).
   E. Illness may occur because God is seeking to bring about repentance (1Corinthtians 5:5).
   F. Illness may occur because God is using it to prevent a person from sinning (2Corinthains 12:7).
   G. Illness may occur as natural consequence of not taking care of one's body as designed (Proverbs 19:16).
   H. Illness may occur as a result of unbiblical thinking and actions (2Chronicles 26:19).
   I. Illness can be used by God to bring Glory to Himself (John 11:1-4).
   J. Illness can be used by God to expose the character of a person (Job 2:1-6).

II. Key Perspectives to consider for the person struggling with a Physical Illness
   A. There must be biblical understanding of physical illness (Romans 12:2).
   B. God has the physical illness under His Sovereign control (Ecclesiastes 7:13-14).
   C. God will not allow physical illness to rise above what one can handle (1Corinthians 10:13).
   D. God will give what is needed so a person can function as God commanded in spite of the physical sickness (2Corinthains 9:8).
   E. God wants a person to be victorious not a victim in their response to physical sickness (1Corinthains 15:57, Job 1:1-2:10).

III. An Approach to Help people with Physical Illness
   A. Help the counselee to see God's perspective on illness.
   B. Help the counselee to focus more on becoming like Christ as the primary goal and getting over the illness as the secondary goal.
   C. Teach the counselee how use God's grace to function responsibly even when they feel horrible.
   D. Teach the counselee how to be thankful even when they feel terrible.
   E. Teach the counselee to focus on victory above relief.

The Distinction between the Material and Immaterial Aspects of Man/Psychotropic Drugs

(Insights from section adapted from <u>The Heart of Man and The Mental Disorders</u> by Rich Thomson)

Key Point: *God's Word reveals that man's inner mental soundness is directly connected to those things for which he is responsible to God in his immaterial being, not with those things for which he is not responsible. (Human wisdom blames the brain for that which the Bible holds the heart responsible.)*

IV. As created in the image of God, man, until death, is an inseparable unity of the material (Body and brain) and the immaterial (heart- or soul and spirit)

    A. We have been designed with a mind which involves our thoughts, beliefs, understanding, memory, judgment, imaginations, discernment and conscience (See Proverbs 23:7, Romans 12:2-3, Romans 2:15-16, Mark 2:6, 2Corinthians 10:5).

    B. We have been designed with affections which involves our longings, desires, and feelings (See Psalm 20:4, Ecclesiastes 7:9, 11:9, Psalm 73:7, James 3:14, Hebrews 12:3, Joshua 14:8).

    C. We have been designed with a will which involves our ability to choose and determine action (See Deuteronomy 30:19, Joshua 24:15, Psalm 25:12, Ecclesiastes 2:4-8).

    D. Our mind, affections, and will, are the sum total of what we call the immaterial part of man(non-physical); The bible generally uses the words soul, spirit, and heart when speaking of the immaterial aspect of man (See 1Corinthains 2:11, Roman 8:16, and Proverbs 4:23) (Sometimes the word soul is used to describe the whole person both material and immaterial (Acts 2:41)

    E. We have been designed with a physical body which is the home of the immaterial part of us (See 2Corinthains5:1-10, Philippians1:19-23, 1Corinthains9:27, and 1Corinthians 15:35-58).

    F. The physical body and immaterial part of man are an inseparable union while man is alive on earth (See Genesis 2:7, 1Corinthians 15:35-38, Philippians 1:19-23).

    G. We have been created as an eternal being that will live forever either in fellowship with God or in eternal damnation (See Luke 16:19-31, John 3:36, and Revelation 20:11-15).

    H. We are accountable to God for our thoughts, words, and deeds (See 2Corinthians 5:10, Romans 14:10-12, and Ecclesiastes 12:13-14).

I.   There is a distinction between the heart (soul and spirit) and the body; the heart (soul and spirit) is the real you and the body is the house in which the real you lives (See Genesis 1:26, 2 Corinthians 5:6-10, and Philippians 1:19-23).

V. Inside man's immaterial heart, is his individual personality which is not confined to his material body and brain. Our individual personality keeps on living even after we die (See Revelation 6:9-11, 1 Samuel 28:15-19, Luke 16:23-31; 9:28-31).

The Personality of Man

Read and analyze these Scriptures: Revelation 6:9-11, Luke 9:28-31, and make a list of things which are usually associated with man's brain but which in these instances are exhibited by people who are physically dead and have only their immaterial beings to account for them:

Characteristics normally tied to the brain of the living:

A.

B.

C.

D.

E.

F.

G.

H.

I.

J.

K.

L.

M.

N.

O.

Key Point: After doing the observation we find that many of those characteristics we assume are limited to the brain are not. Man's immaterial heart interfaces with his material brain while he functions on earth. After death many functions we associate with the brain continue in operation in man's immaterial being. The heart chooses and the brain is involved, but it is the heart that drives the choices not the brain. Man's immaterial heart is the control center of those things for which man is responsible to God. Inside man's immaterial heart is his individual personality which is not confined to his material body and brain. Our individual personality keeps on living even after we die (Revelation 6:9-11, 1 Samuel 28:15-19, Luke 9:28-31)

V. Man's immaterial heart interfaces with his material brain in the area of thought. We need both the immaterial heart and material brain for the thought process to happen while we are living. Thought processes go on in the immaterial heart and the material brain while we are living. When we die thought processes continue in the immaterial heart.

    A. Daniel 2:28 (He was thinking thoughts in his material brain.)
    B. Daniel 2:30 (He was thinking thoughts in immaterial heart.)
    C. Song of Solomon 5:2 (Mind was awake while brain was unconscious.)

VII. Man's material body and brain may limit or expand his ability to think or experience things here on earth, but the body and brain do not determine those thoughts, words, or actions which man is responsible before God to choose in his immaterial heart. Some of us have great intellect, small intellect, and some are retarded but these issues do not affect the processes of the immaterial heart. Sin is not caused by the brain or brain chemicals but by the thought processes of the immaterial heart. Therefore, if there is an issue of sin in our lives we must blame the immaterial heart and not the material body and brain. Medicine may deal with the symptoms of the problem but not root issues (See Matthew 15:17-20, Mark 7:18-23, Proverbs 4:23, Philippians 4:8, Galatians 5:19-23, Proverbs 18:14, 1 Corinthians 10:13).

(Insights from this section adapted from <u>The Heart of Man and The Mental Disorders</u> by Rich Thomson)

VIII. Key Points to Consider about Christians on Psychotropic Drugs (psycho(mind) + tropic (affecting) = mind altering/affecting drugs)

    A. Christians who are on psychotropic drugs may be focused more on feeling better through the medication than becoming better through the Biblical process of change.

    B. Christians who use psychotropic drugs may not understand how to use the Bible to find God's solution to life's problem therefore they are left to secular understanding about their problems resulting in using psychotropic drugs as the solution.

    C. Christians who use psychotropic drugs may be treated by professionals who deal only in psychotropic drugs to address the particular issues at hand.

    D. Christians who use psychotropic drugs may believe that they cannot obey God when they feel bad; therefore they may believe that the only time they can be responsible is when they feel good by the use of medication.

    E. Christians who use psychotropic drugs may have been told that there problems are based on physical conditions of the body that require medication.

    F. Christians who use psychotropic drugs may not trust in the sufficiency of Scripture to handle their problems.

    G. Christians who use psychotropic drugs may not understand or accept why and how God uses pain and trials to build character.

IX. Biblical Perspectives to consider about Christians and Psychotropic Drugs

    A. The Bible is sufficient to provide everything we need for life and godliness which includes bad feelings that people try to address through psychotropic drugs instead of the Messiah and His Word (2Peter 1:1-11, 2Timothy 3:16-17).

    B. God's goal for our lives is not that we live to feel better but that we live to become better through the Biblical process of Change (Ephesians 4:17-32, Colossians 3:1-17).

    C. When there is no organic basis found for discomfort/ or pain you will find that unbiblical responses to life's situations are the core reasons for the discomfort/pain; therefore psychotropic drugs my deal with the pain of discomfort but it does not deal with the source of the discomfort (unbiblical responses) (Genesis 4:1-7, Romans 2:14-15).

    D. Sin behavior and the bad feelings that follow do not come from organic problems of the body; sin behavior comes from the wickedness of the heart. The bad feelings that follow come from the conscience that stimulates the sense of guilt, apparently uncaused fear, and the desire to flee when no one is chasing. Therefore psychotropic drugs are not the cure the Messiah and His word are the cure (Matthew 15:11-20, Mark 7:20-23, 2Corinthians 5:11-17).

    E. Psychotropic drugs will make you feel better but they will not help you to become better (Galatians 5:16-19-26, Genesis 4:1-7, Romans 7:4-8:15).

    F. Medication is a great support but a terrible solution to non-organic problems (Proverbs 31:4-7).

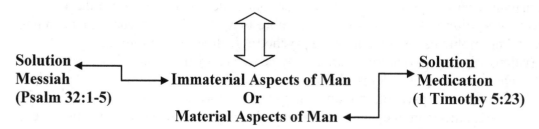

Source of Pain

Solution
Messiah
(Psalm 32:1-5)

Immaterial Aspects of Man
Or
Material Aspects of Man

Solution
Medication
(1 Timothy 5:23)

False Belief about medication and obedience

Pain < Obedience (Lesser the pain/ greater my obedience)

Pain > Obedience (Greater the pain /lesser my obedience)

Therefore, medication is necessary for me to obey God

False Conclusion: Medication brings relief of pain resulting in one feeling better and being able to obey as a result of feeling better from the medication.

Fallacy: One believes that the power to obey is caused by feeling better as the result of taking the medication.

Truth: The power to obey is determined by the Holy Spirit not feeling better as a result of taking medication. Pain or lack of pain does not determine obedience. (Romans 8:1-15, Galatians 5:16-25)

X. An Approach to Help Christians on Psychotropic Drugs

    A. Help the counselee identify the specific situations and problems that were happening to them, around them or through them that lead to the taking of psychotropic drugs.

    B. Help the counselee identify the responses and reactions that took place from them in correlation to the specific situations and problems that lead to the taking of the psychotropic drugs.

    C. Help the counselee to identify the negative feelings that arose and how they chose to handle those negative feelings in correlation to the specific situations and problems.

    D. Help the counselee to identify their goal in the specific situations and problems (biblical or self-serving?)

    E. Help the counselee identify their goal for taking the psychotropic drugs in the specific situations and problems.

    F. Help the counselee to interpret life through Biblical categories in correlation to their specific situations and problems.

    G. Help the counselee to apply biblical principles to the specific situations and problems so that they will focus more on being like Christ instead feeling better in the crisis.

    H. Help the counselee to focus on becoming a better person through application of biblical principles to the specific situations and problems instead feeling better in the specific situations and problems.

    I. Coming off the medication is not the goal but helping the person to handle the specific situations and problem biblically is the goal.

    J. As the counselee comes to see that they can handle the specific situations and problems through the power of God and the principles of His Word whether they feel bad or not they will begin to work on coming off the medication as a secondary goal as you have helped them to develop in the primary goal of the becoming like Christ and handling situations biblically as they walk for God and others.

Key Point: *Illness is a by-product of the curse of sin from the fall of Adam and the result of sin in one's life, yet God can use it for His glory and our good. When you have an illness there is something wrong in the tissues of your body which can be proven by objective test. Mental illness is really not an illness but truly an issue of the immaterial heart that needs to be addressed through the Person of Jesus Christ, the Power of Jesus Christ and the principles of His Word. There may be physical issues that result from the spiritual problem that may require medication but the root issue cannot be cured through medication but only through submission to the Person and Power of Jesus Christ.*

(Information developed from the book ***The Christian Counselor's Medical Desk Reference*** by Robert D. Smith, MD.)

Bibliography

Adams, Jay. Biblical Counseling Manuel, USA: Presbyterian & Reformed, 1973.

Adams, Jay. From Forgiven to Forgiving, Amityville: Calvary Press, 1994

Adams, Jay. How to Help People Change, Grand Rapids: Zondervan 1986

Berg, Jim. When Trouble Comes, Greenville: BJU Press 2002

Burroughs, Jeremiah. The Rare Jewel of Christian Contentment, Carlisle: The Banner of Truth Trust 2002

Cloud, Henry, Townsend, John. Safe People, Grand Rapids: Zondervan Publishing House 1995

Holzmann, John. Dating With Integrity, Dallas: Word Publishing 1992

Lane, Tim. Relationships: A Mess Worth Making, Greensboro: New Growth Press 2006

MacArthur, John. Counseling - How to Counsel Biblcially. Nashville: Thomas Nelson Publishers, 2005.

Macdonald, James. "No More People Pleasing" Sermon

Scott, Stuart. The Exemplary Husband, Focus Publishing, 2000

Shannon, Bill. "Till Death Do Us Part: A Biblical Look at Divorce & Remarriage" Teaching notes (Pastor of Children's Ministry at Grace Community Church Sun Valley, California)

Smith, Robert, D. The Christian Counselor's Medical Desk Reference, Woodruff: Timeless Texts, 2004

The Master's College, Problems and Procedures Course, Dr. Stuart Scott

Thomson, Rich. The Heart of Man and The Mental Disorders, Houston: Biblical Counseling Ministries, Inc., 2004

Tripp, Paul David. Instruments in the Redeemer's Hands: People in Need of Change Helping People in Need of Change, Phillipsburg, NJ: P&R Publ., 2002.

Viars, Steve. "Why Do We Need People" Sermon by Steve Viars 10/03 NANC Conference

Welch, Ed T. When People are Big and God is Small, P&R Publishing, 1997

CPSIA information can be obtained
at www.ICGtesting.com
Printed in the USA
BVHW090534130122
625994BV00008B/663